My
Publisher® 2016

Laura Acklen

800 East 96th Street,
Indianapolis, Indiana 46240 USA

My Publisher® 2016

Copyright © 2016 by Pearson Education, Inc.

ISBN-13: 978-0-7897-5569-8
ISBN-10: 0-7897-5569-6

Library of Congress Control Number: 2015950771

Printed in the United States of America

First Printing: October 2015

Trademarks

All terms mentioned in this book that are known to be trademarks or service marks have been appropriately capitalized. Que Publishing cannot attest to the accuracy of this information. Use of a term in this book should not be regarded as affecting the validity of any trademark or service mark.

Warning and Disclaimer

Special Sales

For information about buying this title in bulk quantities, or for special sales opportunities (which may include electronic versions; custom cover designs; and content particular to your business, training goals, marketing focus, or branding interests), please contact our corporate sales department at corpsales@pearsoned.com or (800) 382-3419.

For government sales inquiries, please contact governmentsales@pearsoned.com.

For questions about sales outside the U.S., please contact international@pearsoned.com.

Editor-in-Chief
Greg Wiegand

Senior Acquisitions Editor
Laura Norman

Development Editors
Brandon Cackowski-Schnell
Todd Brakke

Managing Editor
Kristy Hart

Senior Project Editor
Lori Lyons

Copy Editor
Apostrophe Editing

Indexer
Lisa Stumpf

Proofreader
Anne Goebel

Technical Editor
J. Boyd Nolan

Editorial Assistant
Kristen Watterson

Cover Designer
Mark Shirar

Senior Compositor
Gloria Schurick

Graphics Technician
Tammy Graham

Contents at a Glance

Table of Contents

About the Author

Laura Acklen has authored and co-authored more than 20 Que titles covering Microsoft Windows and the Microsoft Office applications. She has ridden the technology wave from the early days of desktop computers and Windows 3.1 in the mid-90s, to the newest handheld devices and the recently released Windows 10, 30 years later.

While experienced in writing reference books, Laura especially likes writing to the beginner and intermediate level user. She enjoys demystifying what might seem like an intimidating topic—by breaking it down into short, simple, step-by-step lessons. Her friendly, conversational tone makes any task seem less daunting.

Dedication

To the three who own my heart: Benjamin, Lindsey, and Sarah.

Acknowledgments

I'm just a tiny cog in a very big wheel that is the Que team. I want to mention and say thanks to everyone who made this book as accurate as it is fun to read. Special thanks goes to Laura Norman, for her patience and sense of humor; to Brandon Cackowski-Schnell and Todd Brakke, development editors, for their friendly guidance and advice; to J. Boyd Nolan, technical editor, for his careful attention to detail: to San Dee Phillips, copy editor, for her thoughtful suggestions and eagle eyes; and to Lori Lyons, project editor, for keeping the trains running on time and for remembering to remind me to take care of all the last-minute details.

We Want to Hear from You!

As the reader of this book, *you* are our most important critic and commentator. We value your opinion and want to know what we're doing right, what we could do better, what areas you'd like to see us publish in, and any other words of wisdom you're willing to pass our way.

We welcome your comments. You can email or write to let us know what you did or didn't like about this book—as well as what we can do to make our books better.

Please note that we cannot help you with technical problems related to the topic of this book.

When you write, please be sure to include this book's title and author as well as your name and email address. We will carefully review your comments and share them with the author and editors who worked on the book.

Email: feedback@quepublishing.com

Mail: Que Publishing
        ATTN: Reader Feedback
        800 East 96th Street
        Indianapolis, IN 46240 USA

Reader Services

Visit our website and register this book at quepublishing.com/register for convenient access to any updates, downloads, or errata that might be available for this book.

The Publisher 2016 interface includes the Ribbon, page navigation pane, horizontal and vertical rulers, and all the other controls you expect in an Office app.

Publisher's extensive collection of templates gives you a running start to producing polished, professional publications.

In this chapter, you learn how to get started with Publisher and to perform various tasks. Topics include the following:

→ Identifying the Publisher Window Elements
→ Becoming Familiar with the Template Collection
→ Creating and Printing a Calendar
→ Getting Help

Getting Started with Publisher 2016

Publisher is the ultimate diamond-in-the-rough application. Surprisingly, some Office users don't know of its existence, and if they do, they mistakenly think it's an intimidating desktop publishing program. Before you go any further, you should know that it is one of the easiest, and certainly the most fun, of the applications in the Office suite.

There are hundreds of templates to choose from, with more added to the online resource library all the time. There is so much untapped potential to improve the appearance of your business documents, to improve consistency across your presentation documents, and to save untold thousands on professional printing costs. In addition, when you need the quality of professional printing, Publisher can generate a file that contains everything you need.

Note

Because Publisher can run on both touch screen devices and traditional PCs, I use "click" to represent both click and tap, and "double-click" to represent both double-click and double-tap.

Identifying the Publisher Window Elements

For the moment, assume you have *not* used Publisher before and you may be struggling to make sense of the Publisher window. Even if you've used other desktop publishers and you're familiar with the concepts, when you sit down to a new application, you need to know where your tools are located.

If you are coming from Publisher 2013, the new features are all under the hood—they aren't readily apparent from the interface, so you won't notice a difference at first.

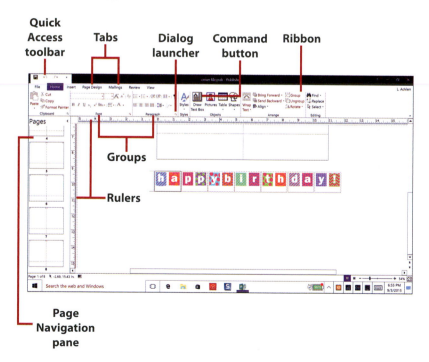

- **Ribbon**—The Ribbon is the thick bar at the top of the workspace. It is composed of tabs and command buttons. You can collapse the Ribbon so that it takes up less room in the workspace.

- **Quick Access toolbar**—The Office 2016 apps all have a Quick Access toolbar. You can customize the toolbar to suit you; simply click the down arrow to open a list of buttons that you can add (and remove) from the toolbar.

- **Tabs**—Publisher 2016 has seven tabs: File, Home, Insert, Page Design, Mailings, Review, and View. These tabs contain commands in a logical grouping.

- **Groups**—Related commands are organized into groups. Each group has a label. All these visual cues help you locate commands.

- **Dialog launchers**—In many cases, a group will have a small down-pointing arrow in the lower-right corner of the "box." This is a dialog launcher. Clicking this button opens a dialog box where you can make multiple changes at once.

- **Command buttons**—Command buttons contain the name of the command and a visual representation of it. Click the button to execute the command (or open a palette of options).

- **Rulers**—Publisher has both a vertical ruler and a horizontal ruler to help you position objects with precision.

- **Page navigation pane**—When you work with a multipage publication, you can move quickly through it by scrolling through the Page navigation pane and clicking the page you want to edit.

Getting Familiar with the Ribbon Tabs

Rather than grouping commands in a menu structure, the Ribbon organizes related commands into tabs that contain groups of commands. It's a visual way to organize commands, and rest assured—everything is still there. For those commands that you use frequently, the shortcut keys that you are familiar with still work in Publisher 2016.

1. Click the Page Design tab. This tab contains the commands you need to insert objects, such as photos, borders, tables, and text boxes.

2. Click the small down-facing arrow in the lower-right corner of a Page Setup group.

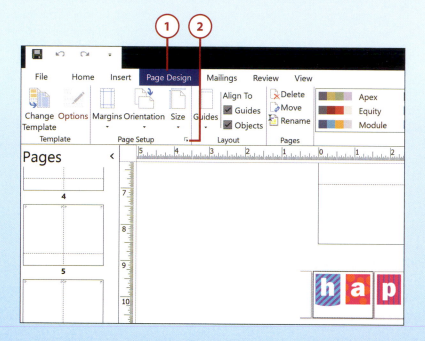

Group Names

Notice that the Ribbon commands are separated by thin vertical lines, which form a box. The name of the group is at the bottom of that box. The first two commands on the Page Design tab—Change Template and Options—are in the Template group; Margins, Orientation, and Size are in the Page Setup group; and so on.

Dialog Launchers

The small down-facing arrows in the lower-right corner of some groups are called *dialog launchers*. The dialog launcher in the lower corner of the Page Setup group opens the Page Setup dialog box, where you can make changes to multiple options at once.

3. Click the spinner arrows to increase or decrease the margin setting, or simply click in the box and type the setting.

4. Click OK to save your changes and close the dialog box, or click Cancel to close without saving.

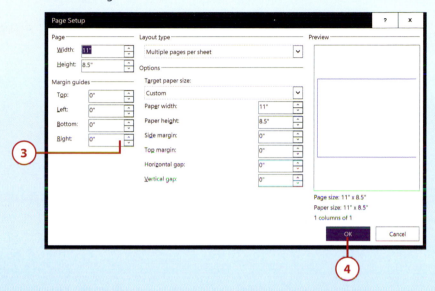

5. Click the Margins command button to open a palette of options. Click in the work area, or click the Margins button again to clear the palette.

6. Click the File tab. This takes you to the Backstage view.

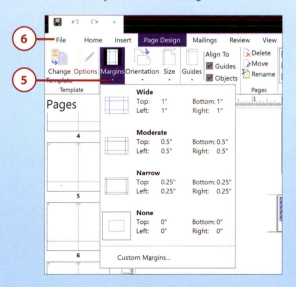

Setting Margins

The Margins command opens a palette of frequently used options to put settings at your fingertips. Simply click one of the options—Wide, Moderate, Narrow, or None—to set your publication margins to those settings. The Custom Margins… command at the bottom of the palette opens the Layout Guides dialog box, where you can set custom margins.

Publication Details

The Backstage has commands to show detailed information for a publication; to open, save, print, share, and export publications; and to make changes to your account settings and general Publisher options.

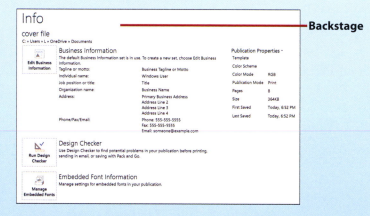

Backstage

Minimizing the Ribbon

The Ribbon is great! It's visual, and after a short adjustment period, extremely intuitive. The biggest downside is the size—the Ribbon does take up more room than a menu bar. At least until you collapse it. Right-click the Ribbon and choose Collapse Ribbon. Voila! All you see now are the tab names. To revert back to a full Ribbon, make sure you right-click in an area between tab names, and then select the Collapse Ribbon command again to deselect it.

Touring the Template Collection

If your job is anything like mine, you want to learn the ins-and-outs later. Right now, you need to get something out and you want it to look polished and professional. So right off, Publisher's superpower comes into play— templates.

Hundreds of templates are available that are built-in to Publisher, and thousands are available online. Adding to that, updates can be made on-the-fly to Office 2016, so there is a good chance that more templates will be added as time goes on, both to the built-in collection and the online collection. Don't even get me started on the user community templates!

Browsing Through the Built-In Templates

The idea behind templates is that you simply fill in the blanks, drop in your company logo and information, and print. If you aren't picky, you can generate an entire collection of business documents with a few simple edits. And if you are, you can turn a well-designed template into your own personal success story as you customize Publisher's templates for your company.

1. In the Backstage, click New to display the New page.

2. Click Built-In to display the templates that are included in Publisher 2016.

The New Page

From the New page, you can browse through the built-in templates, quickly download from a collection of featured templates, and search through the entire online collection.

3. Click Calendars to display the built-in calendar templates.

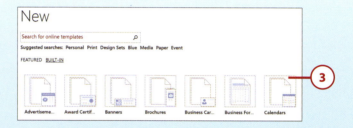

Everything Is a Template?

You may recognize the New page—it's the first thing you see when you start Publisher. It becomes second nature to either double-click the portrait or landscape representation of a blank document to create something from scratch. So yes, everything in Publisher is based on a template—even a blank publication.

4. Click and drag the "internal" scroll box to scroll down through the full-page templates until you reach the wallet sizes, blank sizes, and predefined templates from other manufacturers.

5. Click Home to return to the New page where you can choose another category.

6. Click the Back arrow to move to the previously viewed selection of templates.

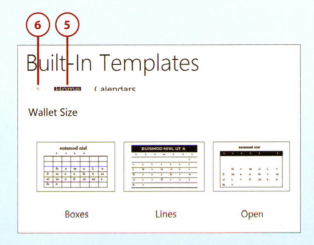

7. Click the Back button at the top of the Backstage options to return to the workspace.

Browsing Through the Featured Templates

The Featured templates are representative of the kind of templates you can find online. When you select a Featured template, you are in fact downloading that template. There are two important items in the Featured templates that can be easily overlooked: More Blank Page Sizes and Welcome.

1. Click the More Blank template to display the More Blank Page Sizes page.

2. Scroll down through the page to the Publication Types and Manufacturers categories.

3. Open up the Manufacturer folder for the type of paper that you need to use.

4. Click the Home button to return to the New page.

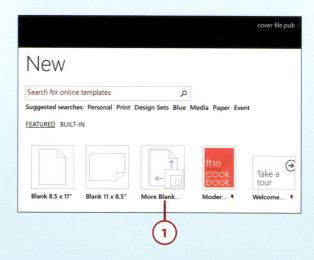

Business Cards

Say you have a page of Avery business cards. Rather than creating the business card form from scratch, open up the Avery folders to locate that business card form. Clicking the form opens a blank page where you can immediately start creating cards.

Welcome Tutorial

The Welcome template on the New page is actually a short tutorial that takes you through the steps to create a vacation photo album. As you move through the publication, you learn how to use some of the new features in Publisher 2016.

Searching for a Template Online

1. At the top of the New page, you see the Search for online templates search box. Type a key word or two to describe what you want to search for.

2. Click the Start Searching button. You see a message stating that a search through thousands of online templates is taking place.

3. When the search is complete, you see a thumbnail picture representing a template that matched one or more of the key words. Double-click this thumbnail to download and open the template in Publisher.

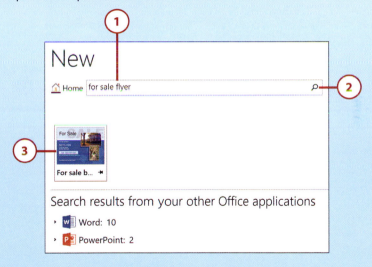

Creating a Calendar

Now that you have a good idea of the breadth of templates you can work with, you're probably ready to use one! A few minutes ago, you got a chance to quickly scroll through the calendars. Now, take a minute to look closely so that you can select one that will work for you. Fill in the blanks and print. Done!

Selecting a Calendar Template

As you look around in the template categories, notice that the Borders Calendar template has a matching Borders letterhead template—and a Borders informational flyer, Borders business card, and so on. A small business might find a theme that matches its vision and begin generating its business documents in just minutes.

1. In the Backstage, click New, Built-In, and then Calendars to display the list of calendar templates. Scroll down through the designs, checking the appearance in the Preview pane.

2. Click the Color Scheme drop-down to view the color schemes.

3. Double-click a template to open it in the workspace.

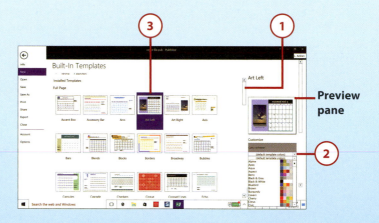

Preview pane

Schemes

While you are previewing the templates, select a new scheme. It is automatically applied to all the calendar templates, so you can see how they will look.

Customizing Templates

Customizing the templates is easier than you think—using Business Information Sets. You can create multiple sets to quickly insert contact information for your company, clients, and associates. See Chapter 6, "Customizing Publications," for more information.

4. Click the zoom slider to adjust the size of the text onscreen to make it easier to edit.

5. Select the caption and then select a larger font size.

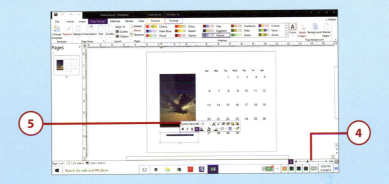

Printing the Calendar

In the spirit of keeping it quick and simple, these next two sections quickly go over printing and saving. There will be a lot more information on both topics later.

1. In the Backstage (click the File tab), and click Print. The Print page appears with the default printer selected.

2. Click Print. The calendar is sent to the printer, the Print page clears, and you are returned to the workspace.

Saving Publications

See Chapter 5, "Saving and Printing Publications," for more details on saving publications, including saving to other formats; and printing, including printing only specific pages and setting up photo printing.

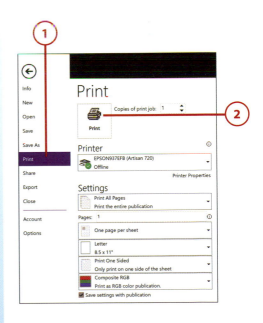

Saving the Calendar

You may or may not want to save the calendar you've been working on. If you are interested in editing further, or if you want to continue to use it as a sample file, save it before you close Publisher. Otherwise, when prompted, choose not to save your changes.

1. On the Quick Access toolbar, click the Save icon. Publisher slides over to Backstage and displays the Save As page.

2. Click This PC to display possible locations where you might want to save a document. For this example, click the Documents folder. The Save As dialog box opens.

3. Type **calendar** in the File Name box.

4. Click Save. Publisher takes you back to the workspace, the calendar is saved, and you are free to continue working or to exit Publisher.

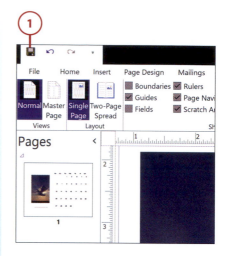

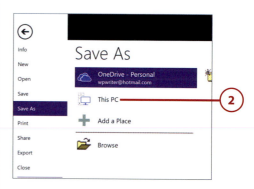

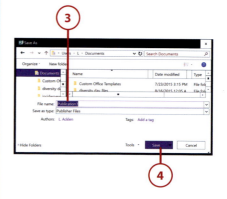

Getting Help

We all need help—especially when we learn a new app or a new interface. Before you feel your blood pressure rising, stop and click the question mark on the title bar and let Publisher guide you.

Displaying Help

The Help window has been pared down and simplified. Simply type a few key words to describe what you are looking for, and then navigate through the search results. Although you can print help topics, you really shouldn't. You can always get back to it.

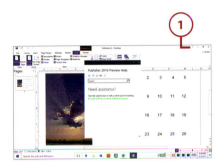

1. On the title bar, click the question mark (otherwise known as the Microsoft Publisher Help button). As noted in the pop-up, you can also press F1.

2. Type a search phrase in the Search box.

3. Click the magnifying glass to start the search.

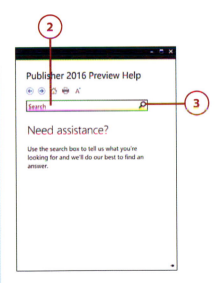

4. Scroll down through the list of help topics.

5. Click a help topic title to display it in the window.

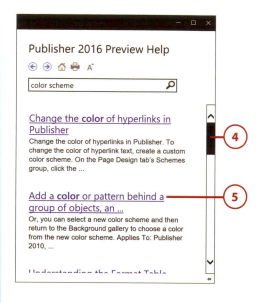

Navigating Through the Help Topics

Reading through one help screen often leads to another. Soon enough, you've navigated through a series of topics and you may want to retrace your steps. The Back and Forward buttons move just as you would expect.

1. Click the Back button to move backward through previous help topics.

2. Click the Forward button to move forward through the help topics.

3. Click the Close button to close the Help window.

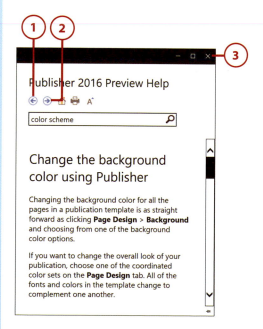

>>>Go Further

WHERE ARE MY GLASSES WHEN I NEED THEM?

Well thankfully, in this case, you don't need them. Microsoft thoughtfully included an Increase Font Size button that you can click to increase the size of the text within the window. It won't affect anything outside of the Help window. In fact, it won't even affect the next help topic. You have to manually increase the font size for each help topic—until you find your glasses, that is.

>>>Go Further

BUT WAIT! THERE'S MORE!

The built-in help topics are just the tip of the iceberg for getting support on Microsoft products. As you might expect, there are "official" Microsoft support forums and boards where you can post questions and interact with experts and members. There are also "tons" of great community groups of Microsoft Windows and Office users. Most people find that between these two online resources, they get their questions answered without ever picking up a phone and dialing tech support. And **that** is a win!

Selecting a different color scheme may be the most fun you have all day! The built-in schemes are inventive and colorful, but if you still can't find what you want, you can create your own!

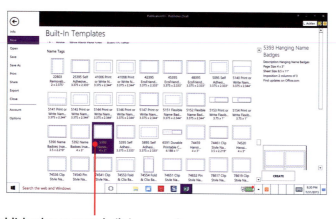

Publisher has so many built-in paper sizes, so you may never enter page dimensions "manually" again!

In this chapter, you learn how to work with page elements. Topics include the following:

→ Adjusting Page Margins
→ Changing the Orientation
→ Choosing Another Paper Size
→ Creating New Pages
→ Moving and Deleting Pages
→ Selecting Another Color Scheme
→ Changing the Page Background

Working with Page Elements

Now that you know you can get a running start with the templates, you can put your fear of creating an entire publication from scratch to rest. It's time to learn how to make adjustments to those templates (or other publications that are available to you). This chapter covers working with page elements.

You'll be pleased to find that much of this chapter will look familiar. Changing the margins in Publications isn't much different from changing them in Word. The steps to change the paper size and orientation are also similar to those in Word. Thank goodness!

Changing the Margins

In Publisher, you don't actually set margins—you set margin guides at a certain position, and then line up items on the guides. Publisher starts out with margin guides set to .75" on all sides. To alter these settings, use the Margins command on the Page Design tab.

1. Click the Page Design tab to display those options.

2. Click the Margins command button to open the palette of predefined options.

3. Click one of the four predefined options to quickly set all four margins.

4. Click the Custom Margins command to open the Layout Guides dialog box where you can set all four margins at once.

5. Click the spinner arrows to increase or decrease the setting, or click in the box and type the setting.

6. Click OK when you are finished.

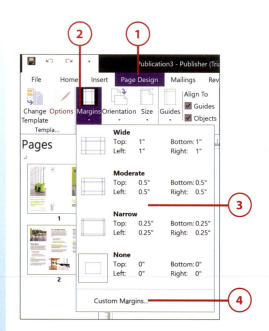

Master Pages

Notice that the Layout Guides dialog box has an option for the Master Pages. You'll learn how to work with master pages in Chapter 8, "Working with Master Pages."

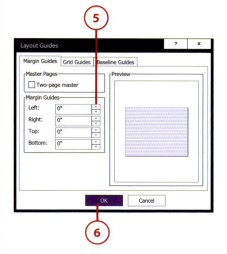

Changing the Orientation

Should you decide that you prefer to lay out your document on a landscape page, you can switch from portrait to landscape, and back again. You can find the Orientation command on the Page Setup tab.

1. Click the Page Design tab.

2. Click the Orientation command button to open the palette of options.

3. Select your preferred orientation and Publisher reformats the page. Your design may or may not be suited to the new orientation. If you don't like the results, just switch back.

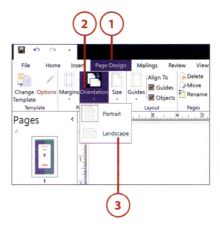

Put Another Way

If you have trouble remembering the difference between portrait and landscape, just think about how a beautiful sunset looks and that you would normally see that spread out across the width of a page (landscape).

Changing the Paper Size

When you start a typical blank publication, it is formatted for an 8½" x 11" piece of paper. You've just seen how you can rotate that page to a landscape orientation, or 11" x 8 ½". Just as you might expect, Publisher supports the most common paper sizes, and the vast collection of other blank page sizes that you first saw in the section, "Browsing Through the Built-In Templates" in Chapter 1, "Getting Started with Publisher 2016."

1. In the Backstage, click New to display the New page.

2. Click the More Blank Page Sizes button to open a seemingly infinite list of page sizes to choose from.

3. Scroll down through the Standard sizes, through the Publication types, where the paper sizes are organized by type, down to the Manufacturers, where the wealth of paper sizes lies.

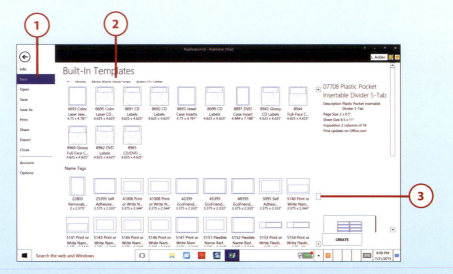

4. When you find the paper size you want, a single click displays information about that template in the right pane.

5. A double-click opens that template in the workspace.

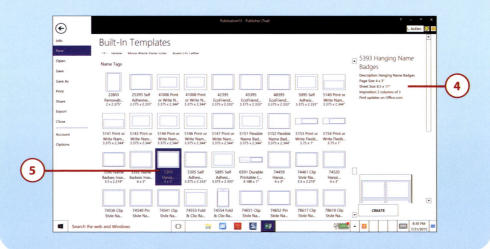

Custom Pages

Publisher 2016 enables you to create your own custom page sizes, so you can tackle any size project. In the list of More Blank Page Sizes, just under the Standard paper sizes, you can find the Create New Page Size button. Click this button to open the Create New Page Size dialog box where you can specify the height and width of the page and margin guide settings, all in one place.

Working with Pages

New pages can be added to a publication with two simple clicks. New pages can be blank, or they can be duplicates of another page. The entire process is geared toward being as quick and easy as possible.

As you work in this multipage publication, you see how the Navigation pane makes moving through the publication simple—scroll up and down through the publication and click the page you want to move to.

Rearranging pages is surprisingly easy using the Navigation pane. Simply click and drag the page to its location, and then drop it into place. Multiple pages can be selected and moved (or copied) all at once.

Creating New Pages

New pages can be added at any time because you have control over the placement, so don't worry about the number of pages you may need when you begin. Add them as you go along.

1. Click the Insert tab to display those options.

2. Click the small arrow at the bottom of the Page command button to open the drop-down list of options.

3. Click Insert Blank Page to insert a blank page after the selected page.

4. Click Insert Duplicate Page to insert a duplicate of the selected page after that page.

5. Click Insert Page to open the Insert Page dialog box.

6. To insert multiple pages before or after the selected page, make those selections in the top section.

7. Now, select from the three options that could save you a lot of time duplicating.

8. Click OK to insert the pages.

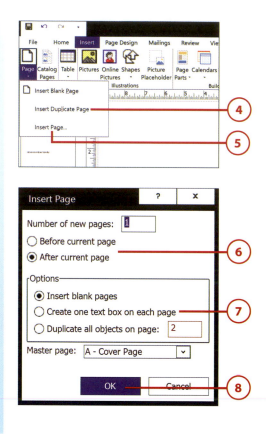

Blank Pages

If you just want to create a blank page after the selected page, click the Insert tab, and then click the Page command button (not the small arrow).

Moving Pages

It doesn't take long to figure out how to move and copy things in Word to save time. The same principles apply in Publisher. For example, say you duplicate a page to act as a model for a new page. The two identical pages are next to each other, and you need to move the duplicate page further down in the publication.

You can accomplish this in two ways. The method you choose depends on your comfort level with clicking and dragging. It's faster to click and drag, but you have more control in the dialog box.

1. Click the page you want to move and drag it down (or up) through the publication. You see a ghost image of the selected page scrolling down (or up) as you drag.

2. When you get to the location where you want the page, release the mouse and drop it into position.

3. Alternatively, you can right-click the page you want to move. This opens a menu of options.

4. Click Move to display the Move Page dialog box.

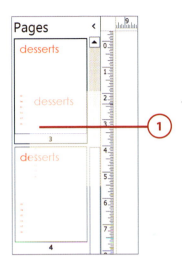

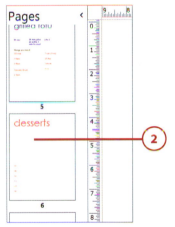

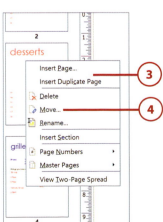

5. Select Before to insert the new page before the selected page, or leave After selected to insert the new page after the selected page.

6. Select the place within your publication where you want this page to go.

7. Click OK to move the page.

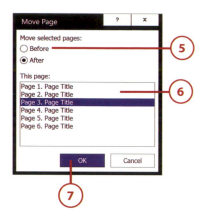

Deleting Pages

As you continue to work with your publication, you may end up with a stray page or two. You can easily deleted these extra pages. Publisher gives you a nice warning if you are about to delete a page that contains objects.

1. Right-click the page you want to delete.

2. Click Delete. If there is so much as a single space on the page, you see a warning message.

3. Click Yes to confirm the deletion or No if you want to take a second look.

Undo Deletions

Don't forget—even if you do accidentally delete a page that has something you need—as long as you Undo (Ctrl+Z) right away, you can bring it all back.

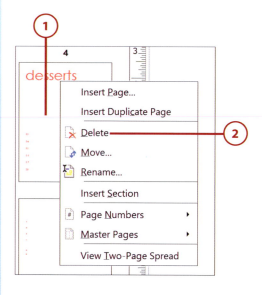

Changing the Color Scheme

A color scheme is a collection of colors used in the various elements of a page. Selecting a different scheme is the quickest way to personalize a template or to fine-tune a publication. There are more than 20 Built-in schemes and more than 70 Built-in Classic schemes, and you can create your own. You'll be like a kid in a candy store when you start looking at all the choices!

Previewing and Picking a New Scheme

As you move the pointer over a new color scheme, Publisher 2016 shows you how that scheme will look dynamically. In other words, as you highlight a new scheme, the publication underneath is updated, so you can immediately see the results.

1. Click the Page Design tab. Focus on the Schemes group. Initially, you see a small subset of the available schemes.

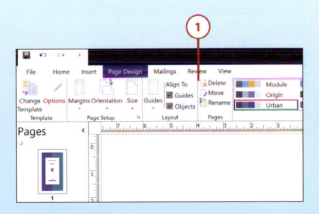

2. Move the mouse pointer over these schemes and watch how your publication is updated.

3. Click the scroll arrows to move slowly through the list of schemes.

4. Click the More arrow at the bottom of the scroll bar to display a large palette of schemes. This large palette makes it easy to see all the combinations.

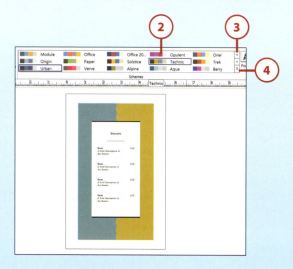

5. Move the pointer through these schemes, to see if any suit your preferences.

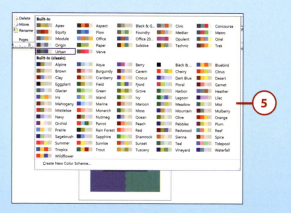

Creating a Custom Color Scheme

If you have a few minutes and a clear vision of what you want, you can create your own scheme. The components of a color scheme are one main color, five accent colors, and two colors to mark your hyperlinks.

1. At the bottom of the Schemes palette, click Create New Color Scheme to open the Create New Color Scheme dialog box.

2. First, type a name for your scheme in the Color Scheme Name box. For example, type **Menu1**.

3. To change the main color in the scheme, click the drop-down arrow next to Main to open a color palette. The current color displays in the left column, so you can compare it to the new color that you select from the palette. And yes, if you click More Colors, you can create your own custom color!

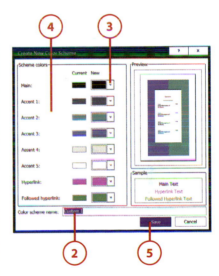

4. Continue opening palettes for each of the accent colors, and if necessary, change the hyperlink and followed hyperlink colors as well. Experiment with different combinations to your heart's delight!

5. Click Save to create the custom scheme.

6. The newly created color scheme is shown at the top of the list.

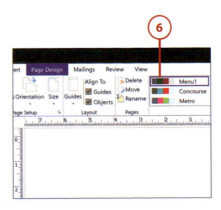

>>>*Go Further*

MORE WAYS TO USE THEMES

Freelancers often tailor their work to match a client's logo—colors and all. It's not uncommon for a freelance writer to play around with the color wheel, creating custom colors to match materials that their clients have already had professionally produced. Having these tools available in Publisher 2016 makes it possible for a small businessperson to offer an economical alternative to "professional design services."

Changing the Page Background

Setting a page background is a small, important detail. It adds another level of luxury to the publication. Publisher 2016 has a great collection of built-in backgrounds that are solid and in gradient patterns. And here as well, you can create your own custom background. Honestly, with all the customizing you can do, it's a wonder you get any work done at all!

Selecting a Page Background

The Background button is in the Page Background group on the Page Design tab. The Publisher 2016 interface includes a palette of options to choose from and a magic button that opens a dialog box where you can select from a bunch of different options at once.

1. Click the Page Design tab.

2. Click the Background button to display the palette of backgrounds.

3. Highlight one of the solid backgrounds and notice how the pop-up identifies the percentage of tint and the number of the accent. Select a solid background from one of the 12 options (varying shades and intensities) to apply it.

4. Highlight one of the gradient backgrounds and notice how the pop-up identifies the accent number and whether the gradient is horizontal or vertical. Select a gradient background from the eight types available.

Creating a Custom Background

This time you create a custom background, but not in the sense that you can name, as you did with the color scheme, but in the sense that you can select from the entirety of the options in one place. Maybe in a future release, Microsoft will add the ability to name the background so that you can use it again.

Selecting Solid Fill Options

In the Format Background dialog box, there are several different types of fills. The Solid Fill option displays the two components that you can customize: color and transparency.

1. Click the Page Design tab.

2. Click the Background button to display the palette of backgrounds.

3. Click More Backgrounds.

4. In the Format Background dialog box, select Solid Fill. The two options for a solid fill are color and transparency.

5. Click the Fill Color button to open a palette of colors: Scheme Colors, Standard Colors, Recent Colors, and the More Colors option, which opens a Colors dialog box where you can pull colors off the color wheel.

6. Click the Tints option to open the Tints dialog box.

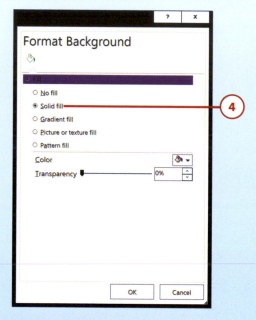

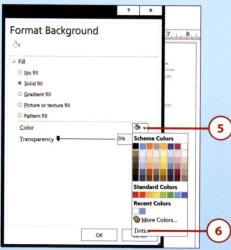

7. There are 21 different tints and shades you can select. Click one of the tints/shades and notice how Publisher identifies the percentage of tint/shade and shows a bigger sample in the lower-right corner.

8. Click the Base Color drop-down arrow to open a palette of suggestions and the usual More Colors command, which lets you choose colors from the color wheel.

9. Select another base color. Publisher updates the tint/shade palette to reflect that new color.

10. When you are satisfied with your level of tint/shade in your color, click OK to return to the Format Background dialog box.

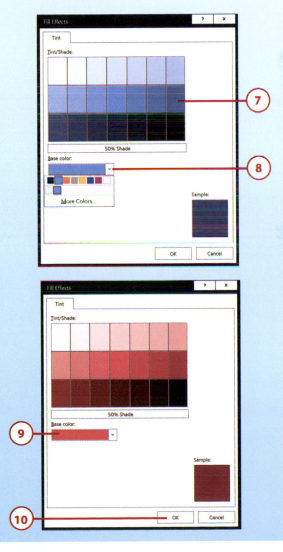

11. Click the Transparency spinner arrows or select the percentage and type your own percentage. A higher transparency makes the background lighter so you can read the text better.

12. When you are satisfied with your selections, click OK.

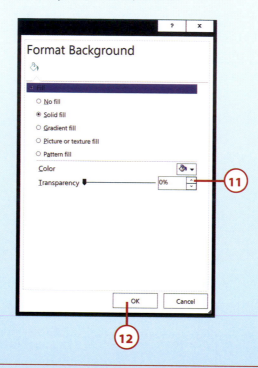

Pick Base Color
It may be easier to select the right tint/shade if the base color is chosen first.

Selecting Gradient Fill Options

The Gradient Fill option has quite a few options that can be set: present gradients, type, direction, angle, gradient stops, color, position, and transparency. Suffice it to say that you can open each palette and drop-down list and make your selections.

1. Click the Page Design tab.

2. Click the Background button to display the palette of backgrounds.

3. Click More Backgrounds.

4. In the Format Background dialog box, select Gradient Fill to display those options.

5. Make your selections. When you are satisfied, click OK.

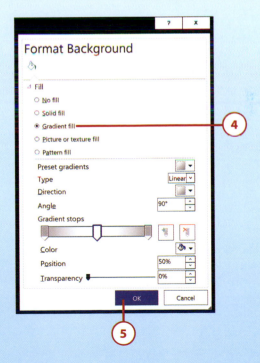

Selecting Picture or Texture Fill Options

The Picture or Texture Fill option does exactly what it says—it lets you select a picture or a texture to use for a fill pattern. It's fairly self-explanatory. The options look a little intimidating, so try to focus on selecting a texture from the palette and leaving the fine-tuning for another time.

1. Click the Page Design tab.

2. Click the Background button to display the palette of backgrounds.

3. Click More Backgrounds.

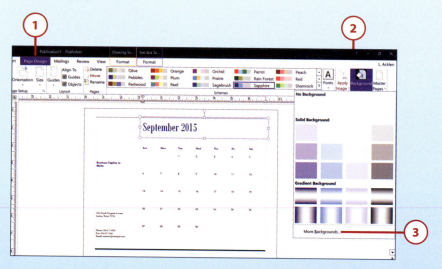

Master Pages

If you want the background that you so painstakingly created to apply to all the pages in the publication, you must make your selections on the master page. For more information on setting up and editing master pages, see Chapter 8.

4. In the Format Background dialog box, select Picture or Texture Fill to display those options.

5. Click one of the buttons to insert a picture from a file, from the clipboard, or from an online source.

6. Click the Texture button to display a palette of choices. Select one of the textures.

7. When you are satisfied with your selections, click OK.

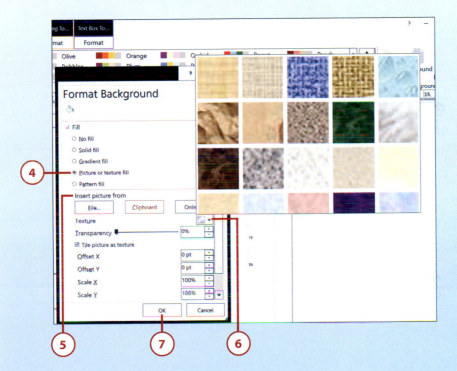

Selecting a Pattern Fill

Applying a pattern fill is actually a three-step process. First, you choose a pattern. Second, you select a foreground color. Third, you select a background color.

1. Click the Page Design tab.

2. Click the Background button to display the palette of backgrounds.

3. Click More Backgrounds.

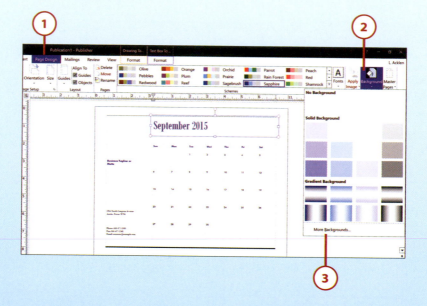

4. In the Format Background dialog box, select Pattern Fill to display those options.

5. Click one of the patterns in the Pattern palette.

6. Click the Foreground button to display a palette of colors. Select the color you want to use for the foreground in the pattern.

7. Click the Background button to display the palette of colors. Select the color you want to use for the background in the pattern.

8. When you are satisfied with your selections, click OK.

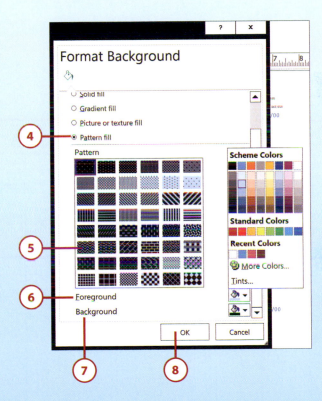

Publisher 2016 has a healthy selection of pre-sets,
so when you format your picture,
it's as simple as clicking your favorite selection.

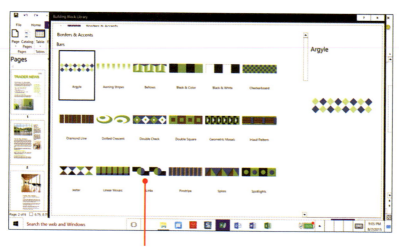

WordArt is so much fun to work with, you may
come up with all sorts of excuses to make more.

In this chapter, you learn techniques for working with pictures and other graphics. Topics include the following:

→ Inserting Pictures
→ Moving and Resizing Pictures
→ Working with the Picture Tools
→ Creating and Formatting WordArt
→ Inserting Borders & Accents

Adding Pictures and Graphics

In Chapter 2, "Working with Page Elements," you learned how to make adjustments to the page elements such as margins, orientation, paper size, color schemes, and backgrounds. In this chapter, you learn how to add and work with visual elements such as photos, WordArt, borders, and accents. Then, Chapter 4, "Adding Text Boxes," shows you how to create and work with text boxes, so you can sneak in some information with your visuals.

Without question, adding photographs to your publication is the most popular way to incorporate colorful visuals. Realistic, razor-sharp-focused images immediately elevate a publication's status and the credibility of the information within it. Publisher 2016 has a powerful collection of picture tools.

Inserting Pictures

Pictures are a powerful way to communicate. They guide readers through a publication by catching their eye, creating interest, illustrating key ideas, and controlling the flow. Key concepts can be reinforced and clarified by using informative picture captions and relevant images.

Think about the last marketing piece you got in the mail. What initially drew enough of your interest to glance at it, rather than just tossing it into the recycle bin? Unless it's an "everything is free" flyer, it was probably the illustrations. Bright, colorful, briefly informative—they communicate as much as the text. Even more so to a reader in a hurry.

Inserting Pictures Stored Locally

When the image you want to use is stored either on your computer, or a computer on your network, you simply browse for the file to bring it in to the publication. In the next section, you learn how to locate an image online.

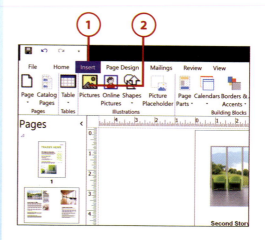

1. Click the Insert tab on the Ribbon. The Pictures command button is in the Illustrations group, along with the Online Pictures, Shapes, and Picture Placeholder command buttons.

2. Click the Pictures command button. The Insert Picture dialog box opens.

3. Use the Navigation pane on the left to browse to the folder that contains the picture you want to insert. If you are unsure how to browse through folders on your network, ask someone for help.

4. When you find the correct image, select it, and then click Insert (or double-click the image). Publisher inserts the image into the publication.

Picture Formats

Publisher 2016 accepts picture files in BMP, GIF, JPG, PNG, TIF, and WMF formats.

Inserting Pictures Stored Online

1. Click the Insert tab on the Ribbon. The Online Pictures command button is next to the Pictures button in the Illustrations group.

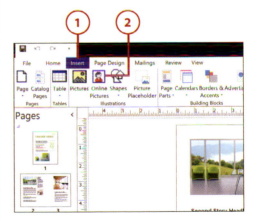

2. Click the Online Pictures command button. The Insert Pictures dialog box opens. This dialog box has Bing search built-in and a link to your OneDrive account. There are also links to help you insert photos from your Facebook and Flickr accounts.

3. Type a search phrase in the Search Bing box, and then click Search (magnifying glass) to get things started.

4. Initially, the search results contain images that are licensed under Creative Commons. There is an advisory to read the specific license for an image that you want to use to make sure you can comply.

5. Scroll down to see more search results.

6. Select one or more images; then click Insert to add them to your publication.

7. Alternatively, you can select an image from one of your OneDrive folders.

8. Click a folder to view the pictures within.

Understand Licensing

The standard warning is "just because you CAN use a photo from the Web, doesn't mean you should." Copyright issues are very complicated and no one wants to "steal" someone else's work. If the image you want to use is not specifically labeled as free, you need to take a few minutes to read the licensing requirements. It may be as simple as adding a simple attribution in small print.

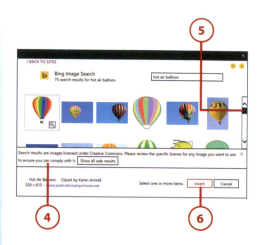

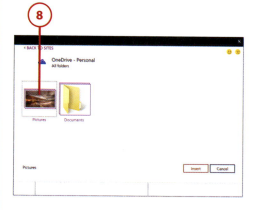

9. Select the photo that you want to use.

10. Click Insert to place it in the publication.

Inserting Pictures from the Scratch Area

When you insert pictures, either those stored locally or those found online, you always have the option to insert multiple pictures. Just as you select more than one file at a time, you select multiple pictures by clicking the first one and then holding down the Ctrl key to click the others. The selected files are placed in a "scratch area" of the workspace.

Using the scratch area, you can get all your pictures open and then drag and drop them as you need them. You can also drag and drop pictures from the publication back to the scratch area. It is like having a white-board on the side with your photographs tacked up waiting to be used.

1. Click the Insert tab.

2. Click the Pictures or the Online Pictures command button, depending on where your pictures are stored. Browse to where the pictures are stored.

3. Click to select the first picture, and then hold down the Ctrl key to select the rest.

4. Click Insert to place the selected pictures in the scratch area of the Publisher workspace.

5. You can now drag and drop pictures from the scratch area to the publication.

Moving and Resizing a Picture

Invariably, you will need to resize an inserted picture and also reposition it. And although that may sound intimidating, it's actually super easy. You simply click and drag a picture to move it; and you click and drag the sizing handles to resize it.

1. Move the mouse pointer over the inserted image until you see the four-headed arrow. This is the *universal move pointer*.

2. Click and drag the picture to the preferred location; then release the mouse button to drop it there. You'll see a "ghost" image of the picture to show you where the image will be positioned when you drop it.

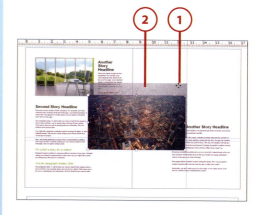

3. To resize a picture, you must first select it. When you do, the sizing handles appear. There are circles at each corner, and squares on the sides.

4. Position the mouse pointer over a sizing handle and wait for the two-sided arrow to appear. This is the *universal resizing pointer*.

5. When you see the resizing pointer, click and drag the sizing handle to increase or decrease the size of the picture.

6. If you want to make absolutely sure that the picture maintains its original proportions, click and drag one of the corner handles.

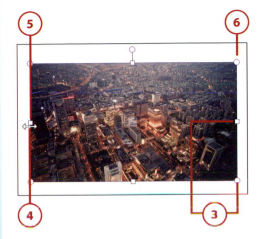

Text Boxes

This was a "quick and dirty" introduction to moving and resizing an image (which is actually a file contained in a graphic box). These same techniques apply to moving and resizing text boxes, which you learn more about in Chapter 4.

Rotating Images

Notice the circle at the top of the image? You will also see this on text boxes (covered in Chapter 4). When you hover over this circle, the pointer changes to a clockwise facing arrow. This is a *universal rotation handle*. Clicking and dragging this handle rotates the image. Notice that as you click and drag, the pointer actually turns into a circle made up of four arrows. This new pointer appears as the image rotates.

Inserting Picture Placeholders

Picture placeholders are handy when you know how much room you want to dedicate to a photograph, but you aren't exactly sure which photograph you will use. A picture placeholder can be moved and resized so that it literally holds the space that the photo will occupy. In this way, you can continue to format the rest of the publication.

1. Click the Insert tab on the Ribbon. The Picture Placeholder command button is the right-most button in the Illustrations group.

2. Click the Picture Placeholder command button. The picture placeholder appears in the publication. You can now move and resize this placeholder so that it takes up as much space as the picture when you insert that later.

3. When you are ready to replace the picture placeholder with an image, click the Insert Picture button in the center of the picture placeholder to open the Insert Pictures dialog box.

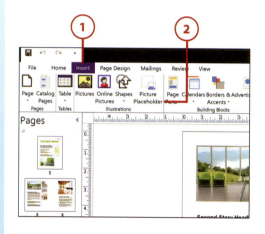

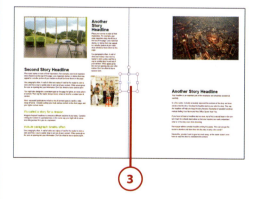

4. Using one of these methods to locate the picture, select and insert it into the publication, replacing the picture placeholder. You can continue to adjust the size and position of the picture until you are satisfied.

Delete a Picture

If you change your mind and you want to get rid of a picture, just select it and press Delete. If you accidentally delete the wrong picture, press Ctrl+Z or click the Undo button to reverse your action.

Browse for a file that is stored locally

Search the web with Bing Search

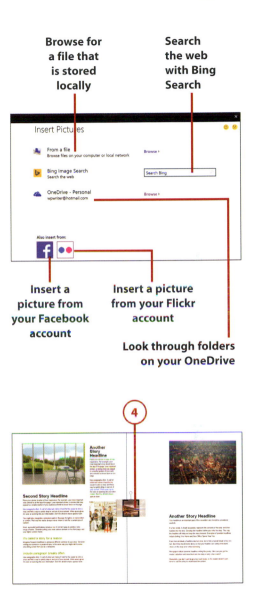

Insert a picture from your Facebook account

Insert a picture from your Flickr account

Look through folders on your OneDrive

Working with the Picture Tools

As you work, you may notice that when you have a picture selected, a new tab displays above the Format tab—the Picture Tools tab. When this tab displays, a special set of commands, exclusively for pictures, is available on the Ribbon.

In this next section, you learn how to use the most frequently used features: creating captions, selecting a style, wrapping text around a picture, swapping pictures, and using corrections and recolor.

Creating a Caption

We all do it—we skim over headlines and glance at the photographs to decide if we are interested in reading further. Picture captions can be used to make a point, not just to describe what is in the picture.

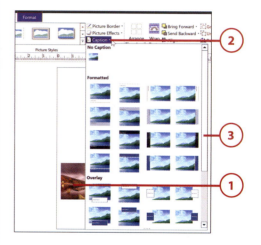

1. Select the picture to display the Picture Tools on the Ribbon.

2. Click Caption to open the palette of caption styles.

3. Scroll down to see the rest of the caption styles.

Style Pop-ups

If you hover over one of the caption styles, a pop-up appears with the title of that style.

4. Click the caption style you would like to use. When you do, a small text box appears below the picture. There are now two more tabs on the Format tab: the Drawing Tools tab and the Text Box Tools tab.

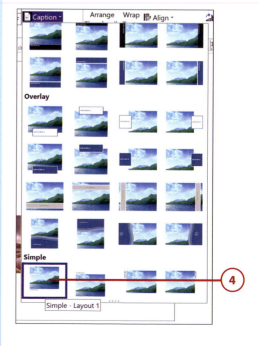

5. Select the sample caption text in the text box. When you do, the Picture Tools tab disappears and the Drawing Tools and the Text Box Tools tabs remain. This is a perfect example of how Publisher 2016 puts the tools you need right at your fingertips.

6. Type the caption text.

7. Format the caption text with the Formatting QuickMenu that appears. When you are done, click outside the caption text box to continue editing the publication.

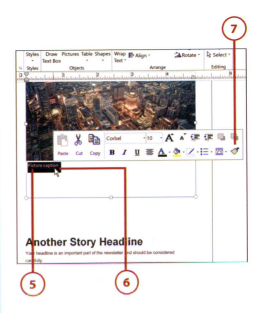

Selecting a Picture Style

As with many design elements in Publisher, you can apply a collection of styles to pictures. Styles are your new best friend. They contain a series of formatting settings that you can apply to a picture all at once.

There are 24 different picture styles that you can preview and apply in just seconds. You can save so much time with styles, you may actually go out to lunch!

1. Select the picture to display the Picture Tools on the Ribbon. You may have to click the Format tab here.

2. Scroll through the picture styles.

3. Alternatively, you can click the More button to display a large palette with all the picture styles displayed.

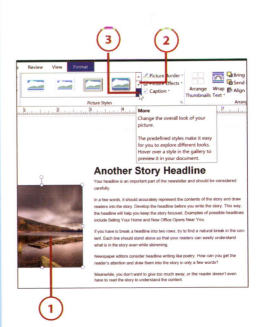

4. When you highlight a style with the mouse pointer, the selected picture is updated to show you a preview of that style. The title of that style appears briefly when you highlight it.

5. Select one of the styles to apply it to the selected picture.

6. If you change your mind, and you want to remove a style, click Clear Picture Style at the bottom of the Picture Styles palette.

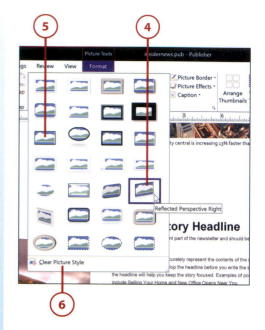

Wrapping Text Around a Picture

Building an effective, persuasive publication is enough of a challenge without worrying about excess white space around the images. And if you combine pictures and text, there will likely be gaps between them. Easy enough—select a text wrapping option, just as you would in Word.

1. Select the picture to display the Picture Tools on the Ribbon. You may have to click the Format tab here.

2. Click the Wrap Text command button to open a drop-down list of options.

3. Move the mouse pointer down through the Wrap Text options to preview that setting on the text and picture.

4. Select the setting that works best for you. Publisher reformats the text according to the setting you chose.

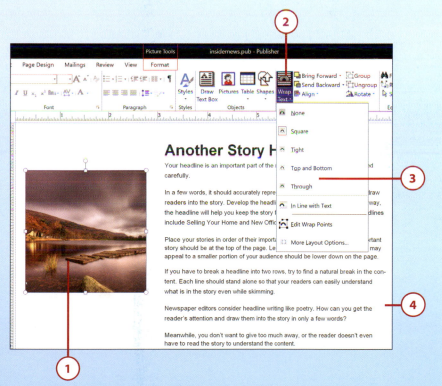

More Options

The More Layout Options command at the bottom of the Wrap Text options opens a Format Picture dialog box with tabs for Colors and Lines, Size, Layout, Picture, and Alt Text. The options in this dialog box enable you to make specific adjustments to the picture.

Swapping Pictures

Well, you've found two pictures that you think illustrate your point perfectly. The problem is you can't decide which one should be the larger, more prominent image. It's so easy to swap two pictures back and forth; you will probably do it just for fun. Simply select two pictures and click the Swap Pictures button.

1. Select the first picture.

2. Hold down the Shift key and then select the second picture.

3. Click the Swap command button.

4. Click Swap to swap the two selected pictures.

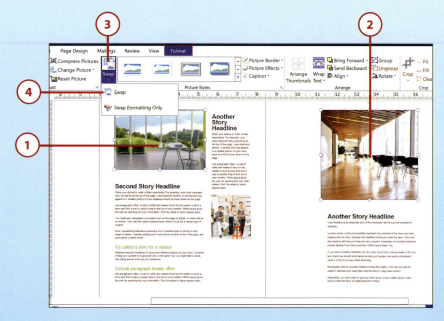

Swap Formatting

The Swap Formatting Only option swaps the formatting that you assigned to the selected pictures without altering the size and position of the originals.

Using Corrections and Recolor

The Corrections and Recolor options enable you to adjust the brightness, contrast, and picture color options. It's a brilliant move to present a dozen options or so, let the user preview the effect, and then allow them to dig in deeper with additional options. You saw quite a bit of this with the page design options in Chapter 2.

1. Select the picture that you want to adjust.

2. Click the Corrections command button to display a large palette with the selected photograph shown with a variety of different brightness and contrast settings.

3. Move the mouse pointer over the thumbnail images, previewing the effect of that setting on the selected picture.

4. The original picture setting is shown in the middle of the options. The currently highlighted option is also selected and a pop-up identifies the brightness and contrast settings.

5. The selected picture is updated to reflect the currently highlighted setting, so you can immediately see the results. When you find the ideal setting, select the thumbnail to apply that brightness/contrast setting to the picture.

6. With the picture still selected, click the Recolor command button.

7. Move the mouse pointer over the color settings to see a preview of the setting applied to the selected picture. A pop-up identifies the name and specific RGB settings.

8. Click More Variations to open a color palette with the scheme colors, standard colors, and recently selected colors. In this way, you can choose another color to use as a recolor option.

Reset Formatting

If you change your mind, and you want to start over, you can reset the picture formatting. Select the picture, and then click Reset Picture in the Adjust group.

Setting a Picture Background

Quite a few options are available for creating a background for a picture. So many in fact, you may forget why you wanted to create the background in the first place. You will recognize the options for a picture background from the steps to create a page background, covered in Chapter 2.

1. Click the Page Design tab.

2. Click the Background command button to display a palette of options: No Background, Solid Background, and Gradient Background.

3. Click More Backgrounds to display the Format Background dialog box. This is the same dialog box that you worked with in Chapter 2.

4. Select one of the option buttons to display the specific settings that can be adjusted for each type of fill.

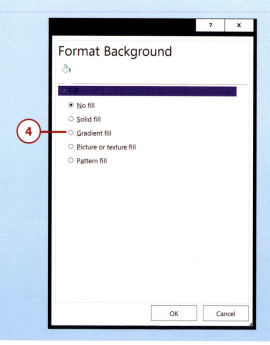

5. For example, select Gradient Fill, and then make your adjustments to the gradient options that appear.

6. Click OK when you are satisfied with the settings and you are ready to apply it as the picture background.

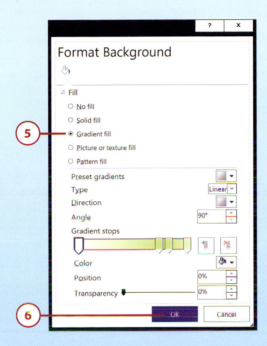

Master Backgrounds

Creating a picture background is an excellent example of the use of master pages. If you create your background on the master page, it is automatically applied to all the pages in the publication. For more information on setting up and editing master pages, see Chapter 8.

Adding WordArt

WordArt does just what it sounds like—it lets you create art out of words. You type in a word or phrase and then manipulate it to create art. The results may not fall into the "polished and professional" category, but the casualness of the result is friendlier, warmer—maybe less intimidating?

Whatever the case, WordArt started as a small utility that you ran *outside* of Word. It has become so popular that Microsoft built it in and continues to include it in each new release. It's simple to use and fun!

Inserting WordArt

Inserting WordArt into a publication is a two-step process: select the style, type the text, and voila! You can then consider that job done, or you can use the WordArt Tools to format and tweak the design. Be warned—a little "minor" tweaking can turn into a 2-hour playtime.

1. Click the Insert tab to display those options.

2. Click the WordArt command button. This opens a palette of WordArt styles.

3. Click the style that best suits your publication. You can always change it later.

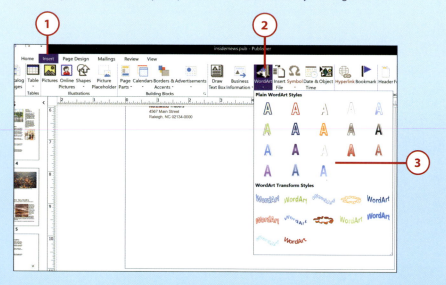

4. The Edit WordArt Text dialog box appears with the sample text highlighted, so all you have to do is start typing. Your new text automatically replaces the sample text.

5. If necessary, select a different font from the drop-down list.

6. Select a different size here if you like.

7. Click OK when you finish.

A new WordArt Tools tab is added to the Ribbon

WordArt formats the text according to the style you selected

Inserted WordArt

Office WordArt

You may have already seen WordArt in Word or PowerPoint. In the Office 2016 suite, it is available in Excel, Publisher, and Outlook as well. The WordArt command button is located on the Insert tab.

Formatting WordArt

When WordArt is selected in a publication, there is a new WordArt Tools tab on the Format tab. The tools enable you to select a different style, change the shape, select a fill, and apply effects to the shape.

1. To change the shape of the WordArt, click the More button to display the same large palette of styles you saw in the previous section, when you inserted the WordArt.

2. Click the Change Shape command button to open a palette of shapes you can assign.

3. Move the mouse pointer over the shapes in the palette to get a preview of how the WordArt will look if you assign that shape.

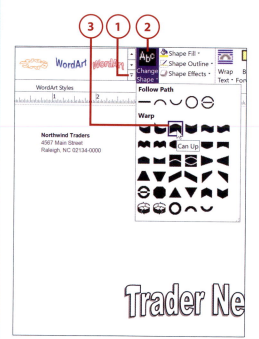

4. Click the Shape Fill command button to open a palette of Scheme Colors, Standard Colors, and Recent Colors.

5. Click here to select a picture as the fill for the shape.

6. Click here to select a gradient for the shape.

7. Click here to select a texture for the shape.

8. Click here to select a pattern for the shape.

9. Click the Shape Effects command button to open a list of different effects that can be applied to the WordArt.

10. Each of the Effects options opens a palette where you can preview and select an effect. There is also an Options option that opens a dialog box where specific settings can be made.

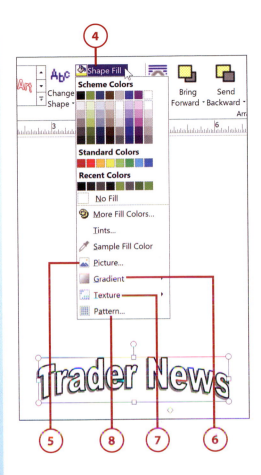

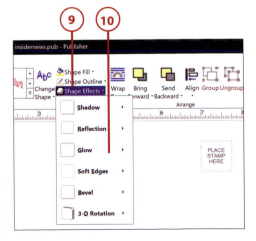

Adding Borders & Accents

Another way you can quickly add professionally designed graphics to your publication is to select them from the Building Blocks Library. Just as a template provides you with premade publications you can use immediately, the Building Blocks Library provides you with premade graphics that you can use immediately. You can find everything from headings and pull quotes to calendars to advertisements to logos to frames and decorative lines.

1. Click the Insert tab to display those options.

2. Click the Borders & Accents command button in the Building Blocks group.

3. Scroll down to preview the Bars, Emphasis, and Frames options.

4. Click More Borders and Accents to display the Building Block Library dialog box.

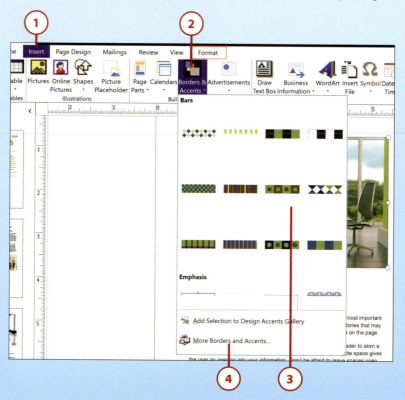

5. Scroll down to browse through the Bars, Boxes, Emphasis, Frames, Lines, and Patterns.

6. Click one of the thumbnails to display a larger image and the name of the item.

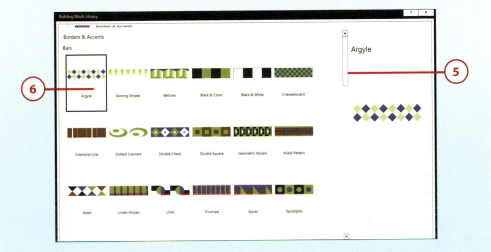

7. Double-click an item to insert it into the publication.

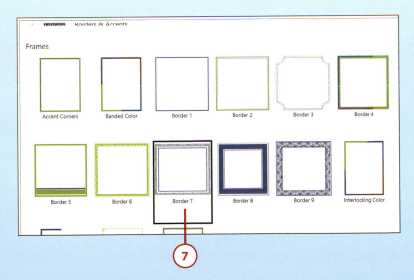

You can link the text boxes together so that the text flows seamlessly from page to page. You can even add "continued" messages to help the reader follow along.

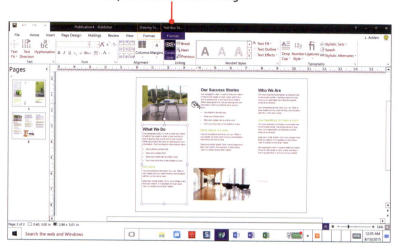

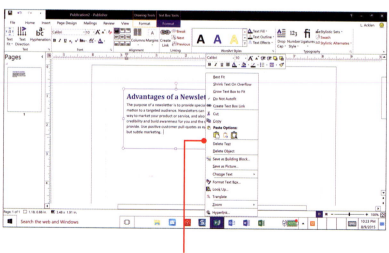

When in doubt, right-click. Chances are there is a handy QuickMenu with a lot of shortcuts for formatting text boxes.

In this chapter, you learn techniques for incorporating text boxes into your publication. Topics include the following:

→ Creating a Text Box
→ Formatting Text within a Text Box
→ Moving and Resizing a Text Box
→ Learning About Formatting Options for Text Boxes
→ Linking Text Boxes Together

4

Adding Text Boxes

Text boxes are straightforward; you create a box and then you type text in it. You can then format the text using the same tools that you use in Word. Publisher enables you to change fonts, font sizes, text colors, text effects, and more. There are also built-in tools for working with newsletters and brochures. You can set the number of columns and how you want hyphenation to be handled. You can link text boxes together so that the text flows from page to page the way you want it to.

The techniques you learned in Chapter 3, "Adding Pictures and Graphics," to move and resize pictures are the same to move and resize text boxes. For that reason, this chapter focuses on the tools that are specific to text boxes.

Creating a Text Box

Publisher 2016 makes it super easy for you to create, size, and place a text box. How? You get to draw it yourself! It doesn't have to be perfect because you can always move and resize later, but it's a good place to start.

Drawing the Text Box

The Draw Text Box command is on the Insert tab. All you need to do is make sure you click the page (to make it active) where you want the text box to be. You also need to have some idea of where on the page you want the box and how big it should be.

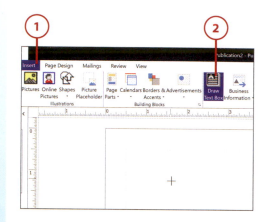

1. Click the Insert tab on the Ribbon. The Draw Text Box command button is in the Text group.

2. Click Draw Text Box and watch how the pointer changes to a small crosshair pointer.

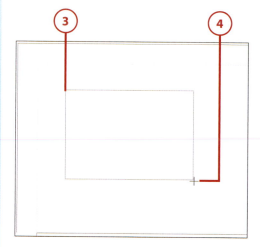

3. Point to where you want the top-left corner of the text box to be, and then click and drag to the approximate width and height that you need.

4. As long as you hold the mouse button down, you can continue to resize the box. When you are happy with it, release the mouse button.

Delete a Text Box

You may end up with an extra text box, or you may just decide not to create it right now. Whatever the reason, to delete a text box, select it and press Delete.

Entering the Text

Depending on the project, entering the text can be the easiest part or the hardest. Writing interesting content can be a challenge, as is combining information from different sources into a cohesive message. When you have the text inside the text box, you can format it to your heart's content.

1. With the insertion point blinking inside the text box, start typing your text. It wraps within the confines of the box.

2. To paste text from another source, make sure the insertion point is inside the text box before you select Paste. (Press Ctrl+V.)

Formatting the Text

When you are ready to format the text within the text box, click the new Text Box Tools tab that appears on the Ribbon any time the insertion point is inside a text box. Nifty, isn't it?

Remember, this is just like formatting text in a Word document. Select the text first, and then apply the formatting.

1. To change the font, select the text, and then click the Font arrow to select a new font.

2. To change the size of the text, select the text, and then click the Font Size arrow to select a new font size.

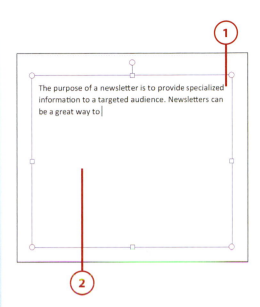

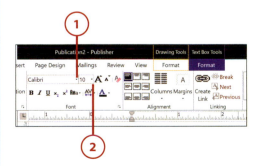

3. Alternatively, you can click the Increase Font Size and Decrease Font Size buttons to make small changes quickly.

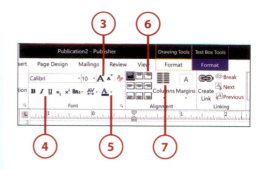

4. Use these buttons to apply bold, italics, underline, superscript, and subscript.

5. Click the Font Color arrow to select a color for the text.

6. Click one of these nine options to align the text within the text box.

7. Click the Columns command button to add or remove columns so that your text is formatted into columns within the text box.

Clear Formatting

Publisher has a great, little shortcut for clearing all the text formatting at once. Located in the upper-right corner of the Font group, the Clear All Formatting button transforms highly formatted text into Plain-Jane normal text in just one click. (Well, you do have to select the text first!)

Link Text Boxes

If you want to work with columns, you will ultimately have more flexibility with the content if you use two skinny text boxes, each with a single column of text. You can link the two text boxes together and then let the text flow between them. You learn how to do this in a later section, so stay tuned.

Moving and Resizing the Box

It never fails—as soon as you start formatting the text, the way it wraps inside the text box changes, sometimes with undesirable results. Or you make a couple adjustments and the text box shifts too far down on the page.

1. If you haven't already, select the text box so that the sizing handles appear.

2. Hover over one of the sizing handles until the pointer changes to a two-headed arrow. You will recognize this as the universal resizing pointer (and from Chapter 3 when you learned how to resize pictures).

3. Click and drag the sizing handle to resize the text box. As you click and drag, a ghost line appears to show you how big the text box will be when you release the mouse pointer.

4. When you're happy with the new size, release the mouse button. Publisher automatically reformats the text within the larger box.

5. Now, move the text box away from the left margin (marked with the faint line). With the box still selected, hover over a border until you see the four-sided arrow. This is the universal move pointer.

6. Click and drag the text box to a new location on the page. When you are satisfied, release the mouse button to drop the box.

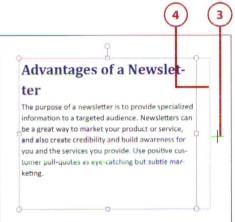

Formatting Text Boxes

Publisher 2016 does a marvelous job of putting the commands you need for a specific task all together in one place. Formatting text boxes is an excellent example of this. Rather than going to a half dozen different places to set all the options, you can do it in one dialog box: the Format Text Box dialog box.

Here, you can format the lines, set an exact size, set a specific position on a page, select a wrapping style, and include nifty "Continued on page" and "Continued from page" messages so that the reader can follow articles as they wrap from page to page.

Setting Colors and Lines

The Colors and Lines tab of the Format Text Box dialog box has options for setting a fill color (background) and a border, placing lines on all four sides of a text box, or adding an accent line on only one side. Along with a background color, you can also opt to use a fill pattern or texture.

1. Right-click the text box you want to format. A text box QuickMenu appears.

2. Click Format Text Box. The Format Text Box dialog box appears.

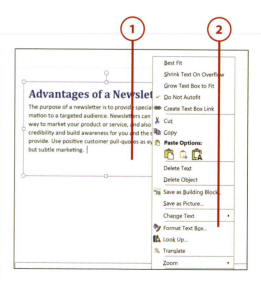

3. The Colors and Lines tab is selected. Click the Color arrow to open a palette of colors, in mostly light shades, which you might want to use for a background color in the text box.

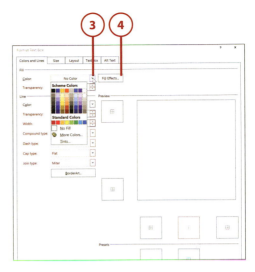

4. If you want to select an effect for the fill, click the Fill Effects command button. This opens the Format Shape dialog box where you can choose from solid fill, gradient fill, picture or texture fill, and pattern fill and then make selections based on that choice.

5. Click the Color arrow in the Line section to select a color for the lines around the text box.

6. Select a Dash Type if you don't want a solid line.

7. Increase or decrease the width of the line (in points).

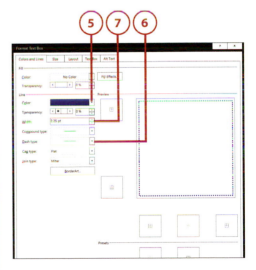

Specifying Size

Clicking and dragging a sizing handle is a quick way to make adjustments to your text box, but for those times when you need to be specific, it's much simpler to type the dimensions in the Format Text Box dialog box.

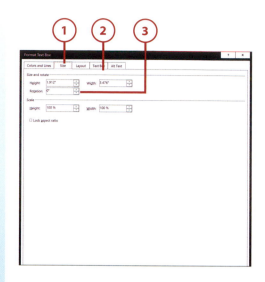

1. Click the Size tab in the Format Text Box to display those options.

2. Either click the spinner arrows, or click in the box and type the value for the height and width.

3. If you are so inclined, you may set a degree of rotation in the Rotation box.

Setting Layout Options

The Layout tab of the Format Text Box has settings for an *exact* position on the page. You can also set the type of wrapping you want around the text box and how far away you want that wrapping to be from the text box.

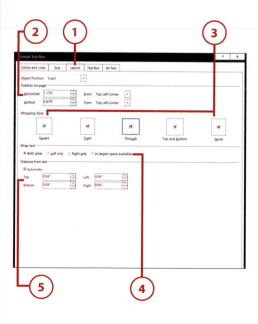

1. Click the Layout tab to display those options.

2. Set an exact position on the page with these options.

3. Click one of the Wrapping Style thumbnails to set the type of wrapping.

4. Select one of the Wrap Text options to control where the text wraps.

5. A default setting of .04" is already in place, but you can make adjustments as well.

Setting Text Box Options

The Text Box tab of the Format
Text Box has my favorite feature on
it—the "Continued" message. You
will love it, too. Simply enable these
options to automatically insert one
or both of the messages.

1. Click the Text Box tab to display
   those options.

2. The text is set to align at the top
   of the text box. Click the Vertical
   Alignment arrow to select Middle
   or Bottom.

3. There is a setting of .04" on all
   four sides. To increase or decrease
   the text box margins, make your
   changes here.

4. Look at the Text Autofitting
   options and select one of them if
   you want.

5. Finally, enable one of both of the
   "Continued" messages if your text
   box will span multiple pages.

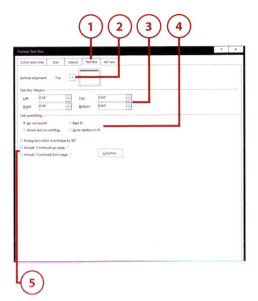

Accessibility

The final tab in the Format Text Box is the Alt Text tab. This is an accessibility
option that is built-in to a text box. You can specify a textual explanation for
information contained in tables, diagrams, images, and other objects that
may be difficult for a person with vision or cognitive impairments to see or
understand.

Linking Text Boxes

Think about your Sunday paper or the last magazine you read. The articles are
formatted across pages, sometimes across multiple pages, depending on how
the advertisements and other stories are combined.

Publisher enables you to link together text boxes, so it will consider the text that fills the boxes to be a single story. Linking text boxes enables you to maintain consistency across pages and gives you incredible flexibility as you edit the text, knowing that it will all stay together, no matter how much content you add or remove.

1. If you haven't already, create the two text boxes.

2. Select the first text box.

3. If necessary, click the Text Box Tools tab on the Ribbon.

4. Click the Create Link command button. The pointer turns into a water pitcher with letters falling out instead of water.

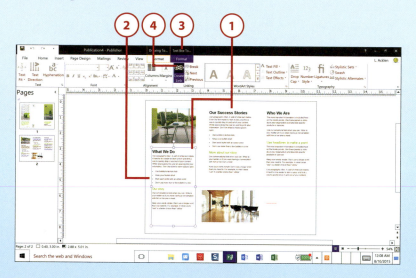

Ellipsis

When a text box has more text than will fit inside it, a tiny box with an ellipsis appears on the border. This symbol is telling you that you need another text box. Create a text box for the overflow text, and then click the ellipsis button. The insertion point changes to the pitcher you saw earlier. Move to the new text box and click in it to link the text boxes.

Break Links

A link between text boxes can be broken when necessary. Click in the text box with the link, and then click the Break button in the Linking group on the Text Box Tools tab.

5. Click the second text box (the box that you want to link to). The two text boxes are now linked.

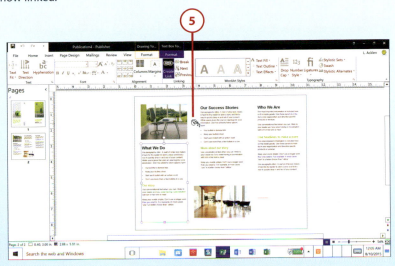

6. When a text box is linked to another, you see tiny arrows on the border: the Next and Previous symbols. Click these buttons to navigate through linked text boxes.

7. Alternatively, you can click the Next and Previous buttons in the Linking group of the Text Box Tools tab.

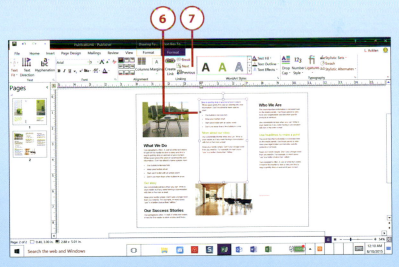

Through the Print place, Publisher lets you preview the publication, select other printers, print only specific pages, print in Grayscale, opt to print on both sides of the paper, and save the settings with the publication.

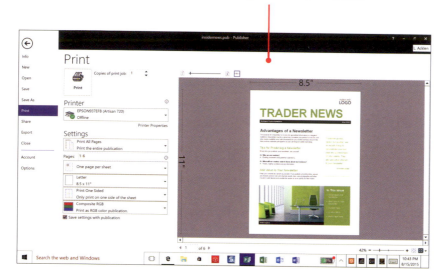

You can share publications in a variety of ways in Publisher, including HTML as shown here.

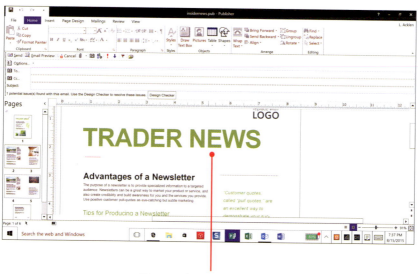

In this chapter, you learn techniques for saving and printing publications. Topics include the following:

→ Saving Publications
→ Opening Publications
→ Sending Publications as Attachments
→ Generating PDF/XPS Files
→ Printing Publications
→ Setting Up for Professional Printing

Saving and Printing Publications

In Chapter 1, "Getting Started with Publisher 2016," you quickly learned how to save a publication. Of all the techniques, that one is a top priority. Until you save your work, it isn't actually secure. This chapter comes back around to saving your publication and delves into the details of saving to formats other than Publisher's native format. From there, you learn how to open existing publications.

The rest of this chapter discusses sharing publications via email and printing. The final section goes over the specifics to set up a publication for photo printing and commercial printing.

Saving a Publication

When you save a publication, Publisher 2016 saves it in its own proprietary format (.PUB). You can save the publication in other formats, however, so that you can share the publication with people who may not have Publisher. For example, you may want to save your publication as a PDF file so that you can email it to your colleagues.

Publisher 2016 saves files in the following formats:

- Publisher 98, Publisher 2000

- JPEG, GIF, TIFF, PNG, BMP

- PDF, Windows Metafile, Enhanced Metafile, Plain Text

- Word Document 97–2003 (DOC)

- Unicode, Postscript, XPS, Rich Text, HTML

There are some important limitations to be aware of when saving your publications in other formats. Saving in previous versions of Publisher is crucial if your collaborators don't have the most recent version. Therefore, saving a file in Publisher 98 or Publisher 2000 ensures backward compatibility, but the older formats do not support newer features.

Your publications may be formatted differently on older versions of Publisher, and the results can be unexpected. You need to take care not to use features that won't be available to your collaborators.

Saving a Publication as a PUB File

Before you learn how to save a publication in a non-native format, go over the steps to save a publication in Publisher's native format of PUB.

1. With the publication that you want to save open in the workspace, click the File tab to switch to the Backstage area.

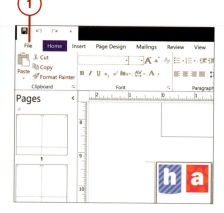

2. Click Save As where you can choose a location for your new file.

3. First, decide if you want to save it on OneDrive or on This PC. For this example, save the file on This PC.

4. Click the Documents folder to store the publication there. Now, the Save As dialog box appears.

5. If you haven't already named your publication, type a name in the File Name box.

6. Click the Save As Type arrow to open the list of file types that are supported in Publisher 2016. You see three Publisher file formats in the list: Publisher Files, Publisher 98 Files, and Publisher 2000 Files.

7. Select the Publisher format in which you want to save your publication.

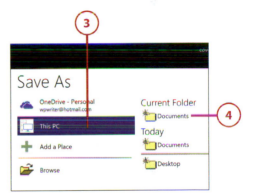

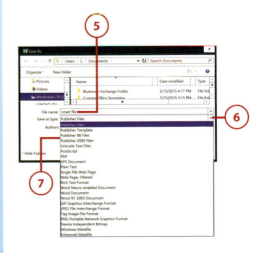

8. Click the arrow next to the Save button to open the Save option list.

9. Click Save to save the publication.

10. Or, click Save with Backup if you want to create a backup file in addition to the original file.

Saving a Publication in PDF

Saving a file as a PDF produces a file that few people will be able to edit (if at all). Which isn't necessarily a bad thing. If you don't want anyone to easily alter the content, saving the file as a PDF is the perfect solution. It creates a small file that is easily shared.

1. With the publication that you want to save as a PDF open in the workspace, click the File tab to switch to the Backstage area.

2. Click Save As to open the Save As place where you can choose a location for your new file.

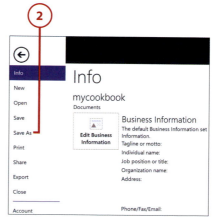

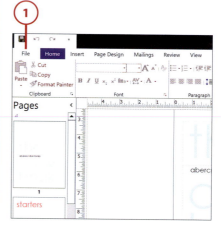

3. Click to save the file on This PC.

4. Click the Documents folder to store the publication there. Finally, the Save As dialog box appears.

5. If you haven't already named your publication, type a name in the File Name box.

6. Click the Save As Type arrow to open the list of file types that are supported in Publisher 2016.

7. Select PDF to display the options for this format.

8. Click to set options for saving the publication to PDF. The Publish Options dialog box displays.

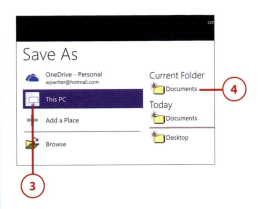

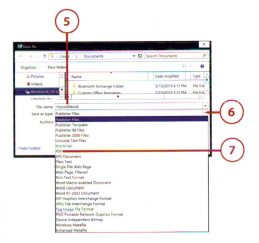

9. Choose the type of PDF you want generated, based on how you will share it.

10. Set options for handling pictures.

11. Enable these check boxes to include or exclude nonprinting information.

12. Enable or disable the PDF Options here.

13. Click OK when you finish. You return to the Save As dialog box.

14. Disable this check box if you do not want to open the PDF after publishing.

15. Click Save to create the PDF. You then return to the Publisher workspace.

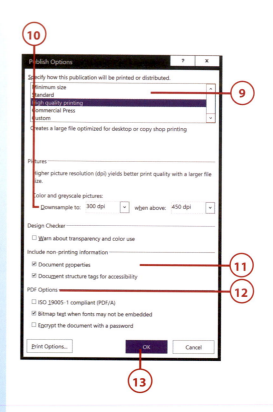

Opening a PDF

If you opt to open the PDF after publishing in the Save As dialog box, you may be prompted to select the app you want to use to open the PDF file.

Saving to a Different Format

If you plan to save your publication in another format (non-native), plan on saving it in the native format (PUB) as well. This way, you can quickly edit the publication when necessary. Then you can resave it in the non-native format if you want.

Saving a Publication as a Web Page

Although Publisher 2016 is not a web site builder, you can use it to save your publication in HTML format. It's so quick and easy; you might think that nothing has happened. Rest assured Publisher has produced an HTML file in the selected folder.

1. With the publication that you want to save as a PDF open in the workspace, click the File tab to switch to the Backstage area.

2. Click Save As to open the Save As place where you can choose a location for your new file.

3. Click to save the file on This PC.

4. Click the Documents folder to store the publication there.

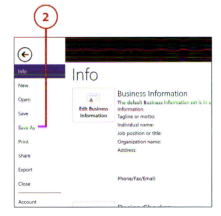

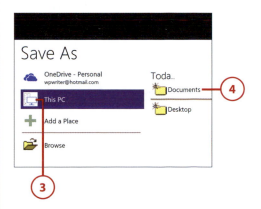

5. If you haven't already named your publication, type a name in the File Name box.

6. Click the Save As Type arrow to open the list of file formats.

7. Select Single File Web Page.

8. Click Save to create the HTML file.

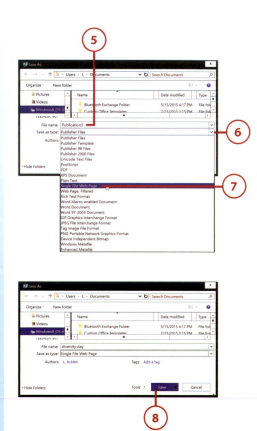

Opening a Publication

Opening a publication is just as simple as saving it. After you navigate to the folder where the publication is stored, you simply select it. In fact, you can elect to open multiple publications as long as they are in the same folder. Remember, you must click the first file, and then hold down Ctrl to click the rest.

1. Click the File tab to switch to the Backstage area.

Opening a File

Regardless of where your files are located, the steps for opening a file once a location is selected are the same.

2. Click Open to switch to the Open place where you can browse to the location of the file you want to open.

3. Browse to the publication file you want to open.

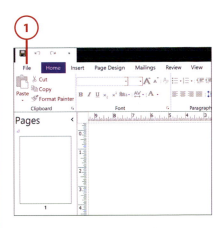

Browse through the folders on your OneDrive

Click This PC to display the files and folders in the Documents folder

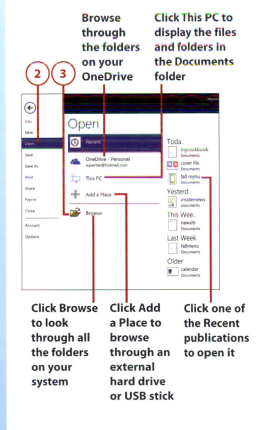

Click Browse to look through all the folders on your system

Click Add a Place to browse through an external hard drive or USB stick

Click one of the Recent publications to open it

4. Select one or more files in the list.

5. Click Open to open the file(s).

Recent Files

When the Open place appears, the Recent option is selected. A list of recently opened publications displays in the right pane, so you can quickly get to the files you've been working on.

Open as Read-Only

You can also opt to open a file as read-only, so you can't accidentally make any changes. Click the arrow on the Open button, and then click Open Read-Only.

Sharing a Publication

Sending files as email attachments has revolutionized the way we work with one another. Collaborating with people all over the world is as simple as attaching a file and asking for input/feedback. It no longer matters if the decision makers are physically in the office, because you can email a file for their approval to virtually anywhere in the world.

Publisher gives you four options for emailing publications:

- Rendering the current page to an HTML to attach to an email message

- Sending the entire publication as a PUB

- Sending the publication as a PDF attachment

- Sending the publication as an XPS attachment

Sending a Page as HTML

When you post your publication on the Web, it can be helpful to share an HTML copy with your collaborators so that everyone has a chance to see what it will look like "live." The Send Current Page option publishes the page where the insertion point resides into an HTML version and displays it in the message body of an email message, ready to be addressed and sent.

Repeat Sending Page

Of course, the process of sending the current page can be repeated as often as necessary to share relevant sections of the publication. Simply click one at a time on the other pages you want to share and generate the HTML.

1. Click the File tab to switch to Backstage.

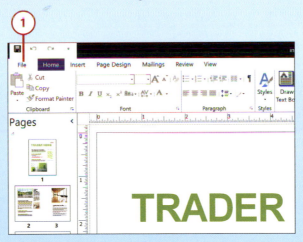

2. Click Share to open the Share place, where you select to send the current page as an HTML attachment.

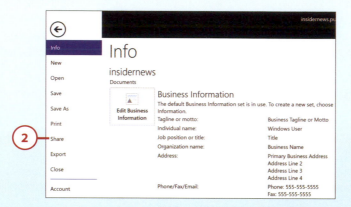

3. Before you share your masterpiece, it's a good idea to preview it first. Click Email Preview to generate an HTML file of the publication, and open it in your browser.

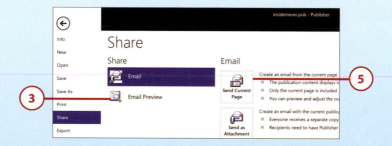

4. Scroll down through the publication to make sure everything looks okay. You may want to do some minor editing at this point, or if you are satisfied, you can send it. In either case, you need to switch from your browser window back to the Publisher window.

5. Back in the Backstage of Publisher, click Send Current Page.

6. In this email message window, fill in the To:, Cc:, and Subject boxes just as you normally would.

7. Click Send to distribute your masterpiece to the world!

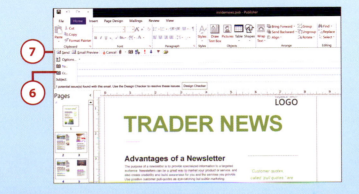

Setting Message Properties

Click Options (above the To: box) in the email message window to set the properties for this message. You can set the importance and sensitivity, adjust security settings, enable read receipts, and set the delivery options.

Sending the Publication as an Attachment

The second option is a quick way to share the entire publication. An email message is created with the PUB file attached. You just fill in the To, Cc, and Subject and send it.

Remember that the publication is traveling as a PUB file, so the recipients must have Publisher to open it. If you have any doubts at all, consider sending it as a PDF instead. They won't be able to edit it, but they can see exactly how it looks in Publisher. That's covered in the next section.

1. Click the File tab to switch to Backstage.

2. From the Backstage, click Share to open the Share place.

3. Click Send as Attachment.

4. If for any reason you do not want to save your changes, click No. Otherwise, click Yes to continue.

5. Click in the To: and Cc: boxes and address the message.

6. Type a subject here.

7. Type the message text.

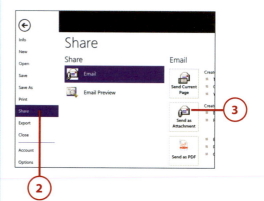

8. Click the arrow next to the Attached box to display the options for attachments. Click the arrow again to close this menu.

9. Click Send to distribute the publication.

Removing an Attachment

If you change your mind and want to delete the attachment, click the arrow next to the Attached box, and then choose Remove Attachment.

Sending the Publication as a PDF/XPS File

These last two options are ideal if you don't want any changes made to your publication, intentional or otherwise. Both PDF and XPS files preserve the layout, images, fonts, and formatting and although they *can* be changed, it isn't easy to do so.

Which one do you choose? If you haven't specifically been told to send the publication out in XPS format, use PDF. It's a universally accepted file format and close to 90% of all computers have a PDF reader installed. So it's safe.

1. From the Backstage, click Share to open the Share place.

2. Click Send as PDF to generate a PDF file.

   Or

3. Click Send as XPS to generate a XPS file.

4.   Click in the To: and Cc: boxes and address the message.

5.   Type a subject here.

6.   Type the message text.

7.   Click Send to distribute your PDF or XPS file.

XPS Files

If you create an XPS file, you see an XPS file as the attachment.

Printing Publications

This may actually be the easiest thing you do with a publication. Printing is printing! You may not do it as often now that we all try to conserve paper, but it's something you should know how to do. Publisher works just like any other Windows application: You pick the printer, set options if necessary, and then print!

1.   From the Backstage, click Print to open the Print place.

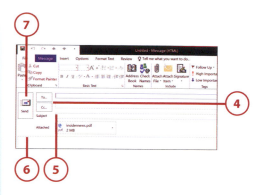

2. Click this arrow to open a drop-down list of available printers.

3. Type the page numbers here to print only specific pages.

4. Display the options that print on both sides by either flipping the page on the long edge or the short edge. Click the button again to close the drop-down list.

5. Select Composite Grayscale here to print in black and white.

6. Enable this check box to save the settings.

7. When you are satisfied with the settings, click Print.

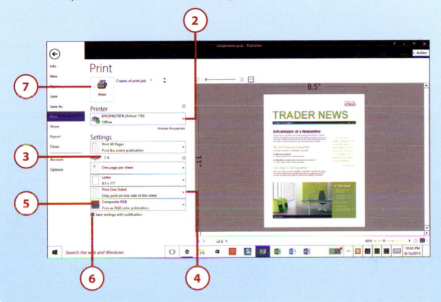

Setting Up for Professional Printing

Generally speaking, it's cheaper to have your publication reproduced by a professional printer than it is for you to print it on your own printer. Understandably, deadlines take precedence, so if you must, print them on a color printer. Most current color printers have a high resolution, so they will look professionally done. Just be prepared for the high cost of replacing all that ink.

Save for Photo Printing

Should you have the luxury of getting your publication professionally printed, you have a couple options: You can produce a file of images for photo printing, or you can produce a file prepared for a commercial printer.

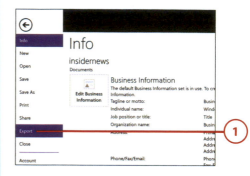

1. From the Backstage, click Export to open the Export place.

2. Click here to save the publication as a series of JPEG images.

3. Click Save Image Set. The Choose Location dialog box appears.

4. Browse to the location where you want to save this file.

5. When you locate the folder, select it and then click Select Folder.

Printing Color Pictures

If you purchased your color printer in the last five years, chances are it prints pictures on photo paper with a decent resolution. They will definitely work in a pinch. Furthermore, you don't have to print on photo paper to get a sharp image. Simply printing on a bright white page produces impressive results.

The JPEG images are stored in a folder with the name of the publication.

Each page is saved as a JPEG file in the best resolution for photo printing.

Save for a Commercial Printer

There are important considerations when you prepare a file for a professional printer. They can only work with what you bring them, so it's crucial that you know what type of file they need and how they prefer to receive it. The company may post those guidelines on its web site, or a quick phone call can usually answer those questions.

Publisher's Pack and Go Wizard makes quick work out of the process. It walks you through the process of saving the files to your desired location and allows you to print a composite proof.

1. From the Backstage, click Export to open the Export place.

2. Click Save for a Commercial Printer.

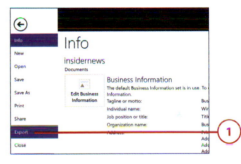

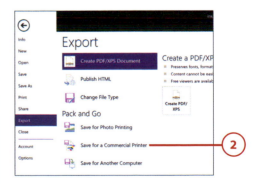

3. Choose to generate both PDF and PUB files or one or the other.

4. Commercial Press is already selected. Open the list to choose a different file type.

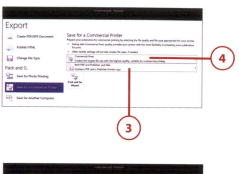

5. If you like, select High Quality Printing instead of Commercial Press.

6. Click Custom to display the Publish Options dialog.

7. Set the resolution for photos here.

8. Enable or disable the PDF Options.

9. Set additional Print Options like printing crop marks.

10. Click OK when you finish.

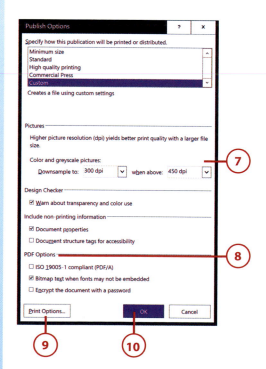

11. Select where you want to save the files.

12. If necessary, browse to the location.

13. Click Next to continue.

14. Disable this check box if you do not want to print a proof.

15. Click OK to complete the process.

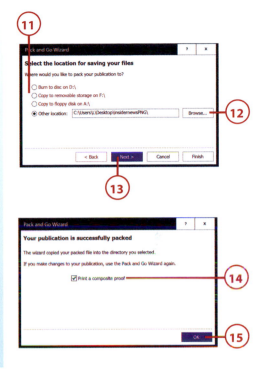

>>>Go Further
FINDING A PRINT SHOP

It's surprising how many people have run into this situation, but just in case you haven't—a professional printing company may refuse to reproduce your publication. It could be that it contains pictures you can't prove definitively that you are the owner/photographer. You could, for example, produce the digital camera that you used to take the picture, so you can display them in the LED for the representative. Or perhaps the shop owner doesn't agree with the subject matter. There are reports of print shops refusing to print anything containing profanity or images they considered sexist. There are plenty of print shops to choose from—should one politely decline, try another.

The Business Information Set feature enables you to automate the process of inserting contact information into your templates. You can create and manage multiple information sets just as you would for an Outlook contact.

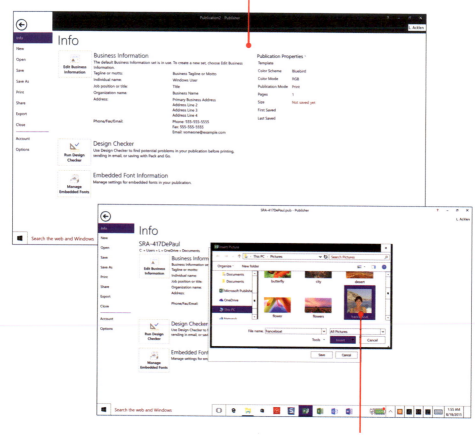

You can use the Add Logo feature to add any image file to a business information set.

In this chapter, you learn techniques for working with business information sets. Topics include the following:

→ Creating a New Business Information Set
→ Inserting Business Information
→ Editing a Business Information Set
→ Inserting a Company Logo

Customizing Publications

You've covered a lot of ground up to this point—give yourself a pat on the back! The Publisher essentials have been discussed, so it's a great opportunity to step back and look at ways to automate the process even more. Most Publisher users use templates to generate the bulk of their publications. Why? Because it's fast and easy, and they produce professionally designed publications. Is there a way to save even more time when using templates?

There is—it's called a business information set. You create one for your company, and from then on Publisher uses it to fill in those pieces of information in the templates. Even better—you can create multiple business information sets, so you can customize publications for clients, departments, family/personal, and so on.

Creating a Business Information Set

A business information set contains contact information: name, title, company name, address, phone/fax, email, taglines, and logos. They are fairly straightforward to put together. It won't take long before you appreciate the time-savings when you see all the contact information filled in for you.

1. Click the File tab to switch to the Backstage area.

2. Click Edit Business Information to open the Create New Business Information Set dialog box.

3. Type your name here.

4. Enter your job title here.

5. Type the name of your company or organization here.

6. Type the full address (street address, city, state, and ZIP code).

7. Replace the sample phone numbers and email address with your own.

8. Type **My info** in the Business Information set name box.

9. Click Save to create the My Info business information set.

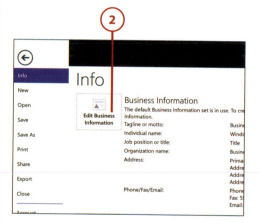

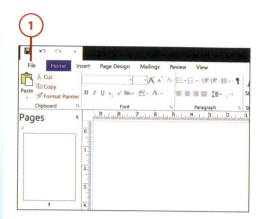

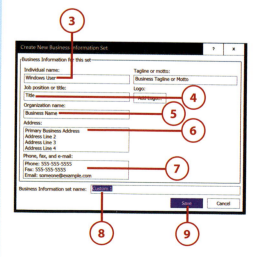

10. Click to update the current publication with the information.

11. Click Close when you are finished.

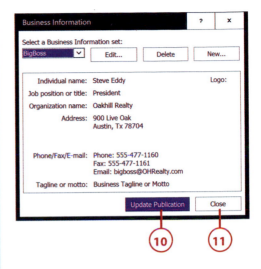

Inserting Business Information

Small business owners learn quickly how to squeeze the last bit of productivity out of their technology. Publisher has thousands of dollars of professional design services built in to the templates.

The more you use templates, the more you will see that the same pieces of contact information get filled in over and over again. Publisher automates that for you, too, with a business information set. You can create as many sets as you need.

1. Click the File tab to switch to the Backstage area.

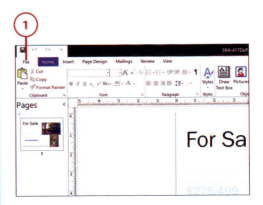

2. Click Edit Business Information to open the Business Information dialog box.

3. Click the down arrow to open the list of business information sets.

4. Select the business information set that you want to use.

5. Click Update Publication to insert the information into the current publication.

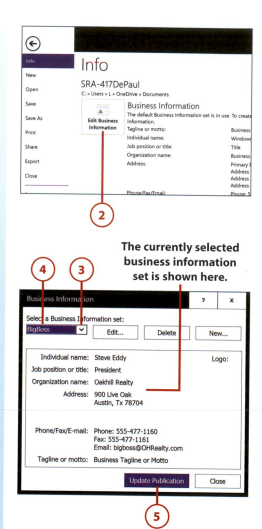

The currently selected business information set is shown here.

Editing a Business Information Set

Maintaining the business information sets you have saved in Publisher is a lot like maintaining an address book. You have to edit the information periodically to keep it up to date. When people change their phone number or email address, simply edit the information set and save your changes. This is not unlike editing a contact in Outlook.

1. Click the File tab to switch to the Backstage area.

2. Click Edit Business Information to open the Business Information dialog box.

3. Click the down arrow to open the list of business information sets.

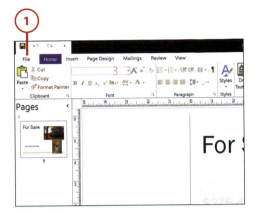

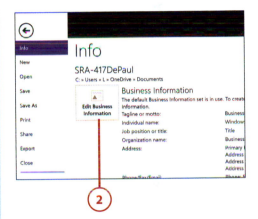

The selected business information set is displayed

4. Click the business information set that you want to edit.

5. Click Edit to display the Edit Business Information Set dialog box.

6. Click in the item that you want to edit.

7. Make the necessary changes.

8. Click Save to save your changes and return to the Business Information Set dialog box.

9. If you like, click Update Publication to insert the information into the current publication.

10. Click Close to clear the dialog box.

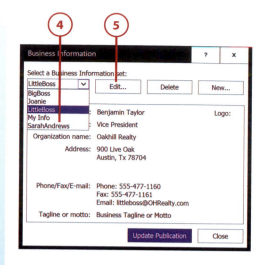

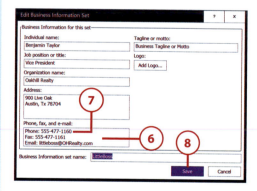

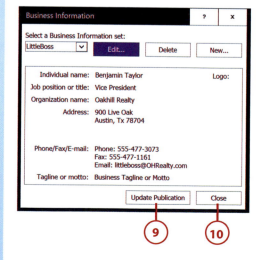

Inserting a Company Logo

Adding a company logo is one of the many uses of the Add Logo feature. You might, for example, use it to add a photograph. Actually, for a busy real estate company that needs to personalize Open House flyers for each agent, adding the agents' picture to their business information set is a great timesaver.

1. In the Backstage, click Edit Business Information to open the Business Information dialog box.

2. Open the list of business information sets, and select the one you want to add the picture to.

3. Click Edit to display the Edit Business Information Set dialog box.

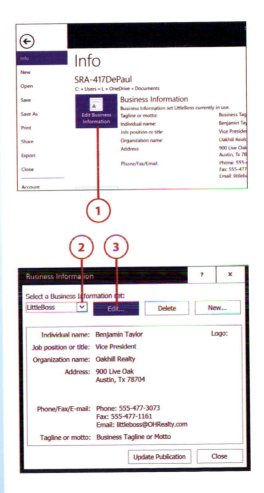

4. Click Add Logo to open the Insert Picture dialog box.

5. If necessary, browse to the folder that contains the picture you want to insert.

6. Select the image you want to use.

7. Click Insert to add it to the business information set.

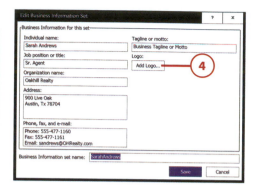

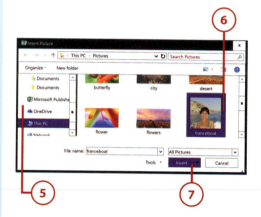

8. Click Save to save your changes and return to the Business Information dialog box.

9. If necessary, click Update Publication to insert the photo/logo into the current publication.

10. Click Close to clear the dialog box.

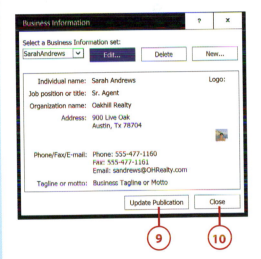

The QuickMenus are especially helpful
when working with tables. All the most
frequently used commands are grouped
together in a palette and list.

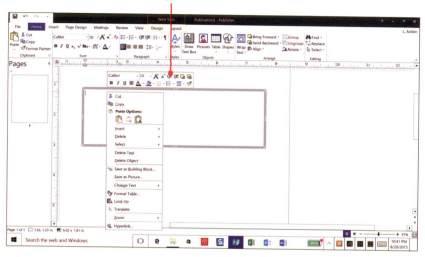

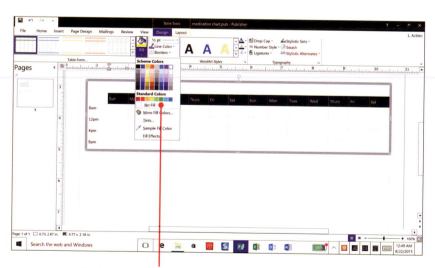

The familiar scheme and standard
color sets are available to be used
as fills and tints in a table.

In this chapter, you learn techniques for incorporating tables into your publications. Topics include the following:

→ Inserting, Resizing, and Moving Tables
→ Using the Layout Tools to Make Changes to the Table Contents
→ Using the Design Tools to Make Changes to the Table
→ Importing Spreadsheets and Graphs

7

Incorporating Tables

Whenever you need to organize information into rows and columns (in a grid), you want to use tables. They are super easy to create, manipulate, and format. In just a few minutes, you can create lists, invoices, schedules, fill-in-the-blank forms, and much more.

The contents of a table cell are not limited to text. Photographs, clip art, and other types of graphics can be placed in a cell. With the ability to print the lines (or not), tables will quickly become your go-to tool for presenting information in columns.

Creating, Resizing, and Moving Tables

Creating a table takes seconds. Planning how you want to set up the table takes a little longer. First, sketch out an idea of how you want to organize the information. How many columns will you need? Second, try to guess the number of rows, but those are easy to add. Columns—not so much. It can be done, but it usually requires tweaking the size of all the other columns.

As far as Publisher is concerned, the table is just like any other "box." You can click and drag it to move and resize it just like you did with the pictures and text boxes in Chapter 3, "Adding Pictures and Graphics," and Chapter 4, "Adding Text Boxes," respectively.

Inserting Tables

There are two methods to create a table: click and drag across a grid, or use a dialog box where you can type in the number of rows and columns. Which method you use depends on how comfortable you are with the mouse. If you have trouble with the finer movements, just use the dialog box.

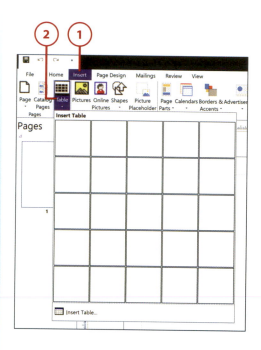

1. Click the Insert tab to switch to those options.

2. Click the Table button to open the Insert Table grid. This is where you click and drag to create the table.

3. Click and drag across the grid to select the number of rows and columns you want. When the dimensions are correct, release the mouse button to create the table.

Table Terminology

Tables are similar to spreadsheets, so the terminology is similar. The intersection of a row and column is called a *cell*. As you enter text, Publisher wraps the words within the cell, adding lines to the row to accommodate what you type. Therefore, a row is as tall as the tallest cell within it.

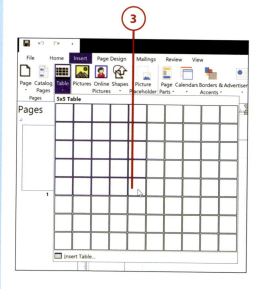

4. For this example, undo the creation of the table so that you can create a new one using the second method. Press Ctrl+Z or click Undo.

5. Click the Insert tab.

6. Click the Table button to open the Insert Table grid.

7. Click Insert Table at the bottom of the grid. This opens the Create Table dialog box.

8. Specify the number of rows here.

9. Specify the number of columns here.

10. Click OK to create the table.

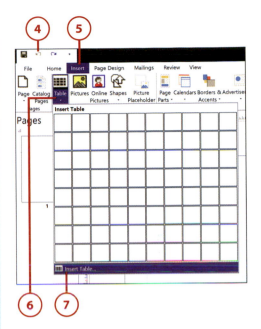

Resizing Columns

One of the first things you'll want to do after you create a table is to resize the columns (skinny columns for dates, wider columns for descriptions). Simply hover the pointer over a column border and wait for the double-arrow to appear. Click and drag to resize that column. Rows adjust their size automatically. Should you want to manually resize a row, hover over a row border, and then click and drag it to resize the row.

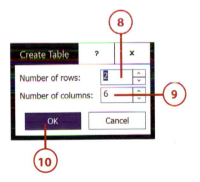

Resizing Tables

It's usually apparent when you start entering the information if you need to increase the size of the table. If you find that you need more room, either for more columns or for wider columns, consider using a landscape page, which is 11" wide, versus the 8½" wide portrait page.

There are two methods for resizing tables: Use the mouse to click and drag the sizing handles or use a dialog box and type in exact dimensions.

1. Select the table so that a thick border appears around it.

2. Hover over a sizing handle until the double-headed arrow appears.

3. Click and drag the sizing handle to increase or decrease the size of the table.

4 Release the mouse button when the size is right.

The Table Tools tabs appear: Design and Layout.

The unprintable lines show the borders of rows and columns.

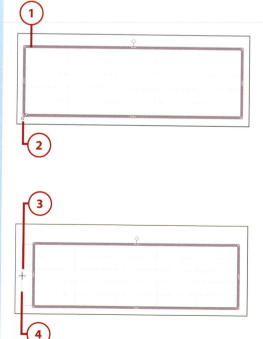

The insertion point is in the first row/column.

The thick line shows the selected table.

5. Right-click the table to display the QuickMenu.

6. Click Format Table.

7. In the Format Table dialog box, click the Size tab.

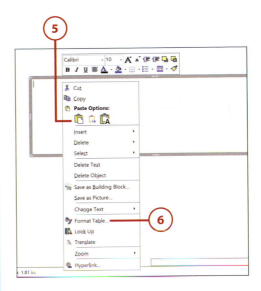

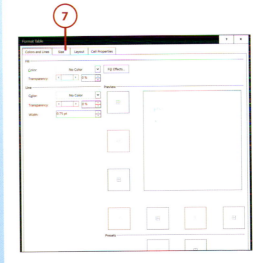

8. Type the height here.

9. Type the width here.

10. Click OK to adjust the size.

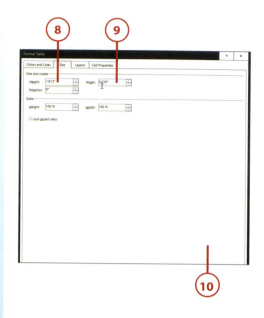

Moving Tables

Just as with resizing, you have a couple options for repositioning a table. The first is to simply click and drag the table to a new location. The second is to use the Format Table dialog options to set a precise position on the page.

1. Select the table so that a thick border appears around it.

2. Hover over a border until you see the four-headed arrow. This is the universal move pointer.

3. Click and drag the table to a new location.

4. Release the mouse button to drop the table into position.

5. Alternatively, right-click the table to display the QuickMenu.

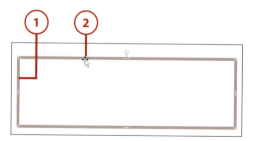

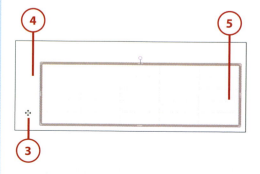

6. Click Format Table.

7. In the Format Table dialog box, click the Layout tab.

8. Type the Horizontal position here.

9. Open the adjacent From drop-down list and choose an option.

10. Type the Vertical position here.

11. Open the adjacent From drop-down list and choose an option.

12. Click OK to adjust the position.

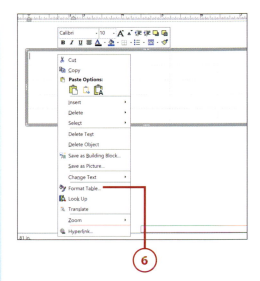

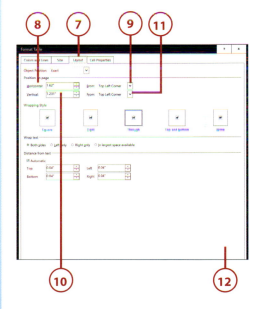

Working with Layout Tools

The formatting commands for tables are divided into two categories: layout and design. The Layout tools are for working with rows, columns, and cells; the Design tools are for polishing the overall look of the table. Specifically, you use the Layout tools to insert rows and columns, to merge cells, and to split them. There is even a command button to insert diagonals in a cell.

The alignment options are used to position the contents of a cell, in the cell. You can change the text direction, which is fantastic when you want to label narrow columns—you simply rotate it sideways and use a tall header row.

Inserting/Deleting Rows and Columns

Sometimes when you start entering information into a table, you realize you are trying to put in too much text. To pare down a table, you can remove rows and columns.

1. Click inside the table where you want to insert a row.

2. Click the Layout tab (of the Table Tools tab).

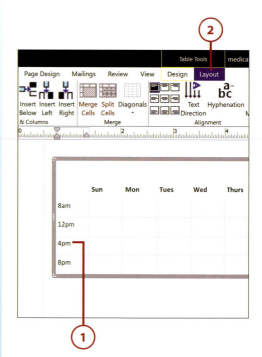

3. Insert a row above the insertion point.

4. With the new row still selected, click Delete.

5. Click Delete Rows.

Undo Deletions

Remember, if you accidentally delete something important, you can always Undo the deletion. Press Ctrl+Z or click Undo.

Right-Click Menus

Some people live and die by the right-click menus. They are handy for frequent tasks, such as inserting or deleting a row/column. Right-click where you want to insert or delete the row/column; then click either Insert or Delete. Click your choice from the submenu.

Insert a row above the insertion point. **Insert a column to the left of the insertion point.**

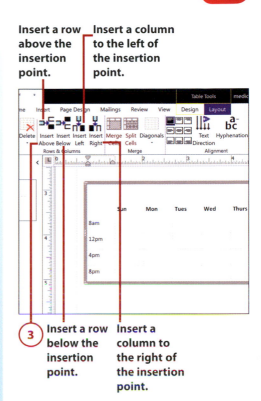

Insert a row below the insertion point. **Insert a column to the right of the insertion point.**

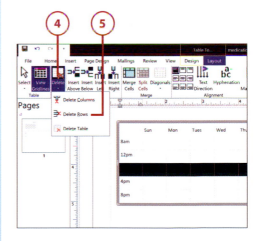

6. Click in the table where you want to insert a column.

7. Click Insert Left or Insert Right to insert the column to the right or left of the insertion point.

8. With the new column still selected, click Delete and then Delete Columns.

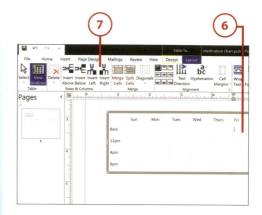

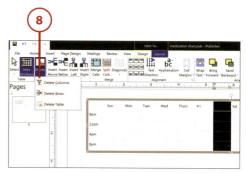

Merging and Splitting Cells

Publisher lets you merge one or more cells together into one big cell. For example, you can create a title row by joining the cells in the top row together. If you change your mind later, you can always reverse the process by splitting the joined cells. You can split only previously merged cells (returning them to their original layout).

1. Click inside a table to display the Table Tools tab.

2. Click the Layout tab.

3. Select the cells that you want to merge (Shift+arrows).

4. Click Merge Cells to join the selected cells into one big cell.

5. With the newly merged cell still selected, click Split Cells to return them to their original layout.

Adding Diagonals

The Diagonals feature splits a table cell from the left down to the right, or from the right down to the left. Select one or more cells, click Diagonals, and then Click Divide Down or Divide Up. To remove a diagonal, select the cell(s), and then click Diagonals, No Division.

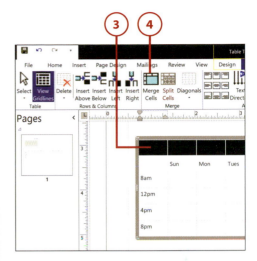

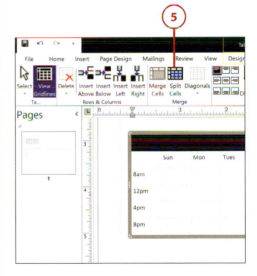

Aligning Contents in a Cell

Publisher makes it incredibly easy for you to align the contents of a cell within that cell. There are nine handy buttons on the Layout tab: Align Top Left, Align Top Center, Align Top Right, Align Center Left, Align Center, Align Center Right, Align Bottom Left, Align Bottom Center, Align Bottom Right.

1. Click inside a table to display the Table Tools.

2. Click the Layout tab.

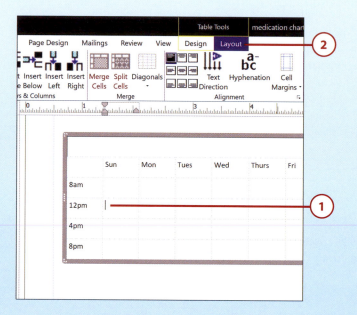

3. Select the cells that you want to align.

4. Click one of the alignment buttons.

Vertical Text

The direction of text in a cell can be changed from horizontal to vertical with just a simple click. Click in the cell, and then click Text Direction. Click it again to switch back.

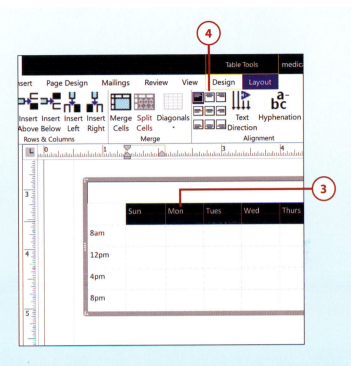

The text is centered with the Align Center option.

Preset Margins

Publisher has some preset margin settings to choose from. Cell margins can be set to narrow (.04" on all sides), moderate (.06"on all sides), or wide (.1" on all sides). There's also a Custom Margins option where you can type in exactly what you want.

Setting a Table Size

Sometimes you need to create a form to exact specifications. If you need to set a specific size for the table, do it with the Height and Width options in the Size group.

1. Click inside a table to display the Table Tools.

2. Click the Layout tab.

3. Type a specific height here.

4. Type a specific width here.

5. Set the table to grow as you add more text.

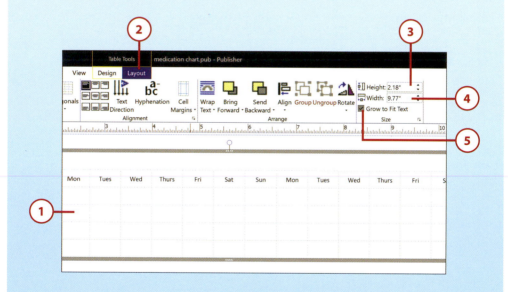

Wrapping Text

The Wrap Text command button in the Arrange group opens a list where you can choose how you want text to wrap around the table. The choices are None, Square, Tight, Top and Bottom, Through, and Inline with Text. These are the same options you saw when you worked with pictures and text boxes in Chapters 3 and 4, respectively.

Working with Design Tools

Up until now, you've learned how to work with cells, rows, and columns using the tools on the Layout tab. In this section, you learn how to use the Design tools to improve and manage the appearance of the table as a whole. By far, the most popular option is to apply one of the predefined table styles to bring color and polish to a table. Other features include applying a fill to a cell or selected cells and setting border options.

Applying a Table Style

There is a gallery of table styles that can be applied to a table. Rather than formatting the lines, fill, and other elements separately, a table style lets you format all those in one step.

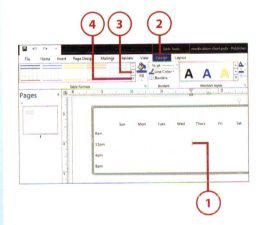

1. Click inside a table to display the Table Tools.

2. Click the Design tab.

3. Scroll down through the table styles.

4. Click the More button to open the palette.

5. Click one of the styles to apply it to the table.

6. Scroll down to see the complete list of styles.

7. Click the dialog launcher to open the Format Table dialog box.

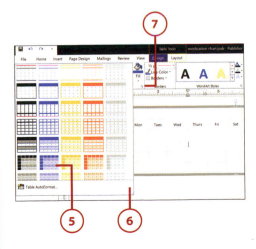

QuickTips

If you hover over one of the table styles in the palette, a QuickTip appears identifying the name of that style.

8. Set the fill options here.

9. Set the line options here.

10. Click OK when you finish.

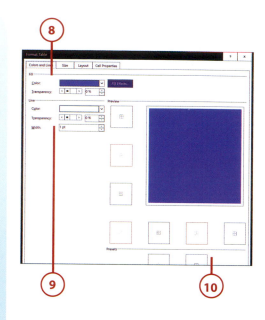

Applying a Fill to a Cell

A fill is a colored or shaded cell background. A fill color can be applied as a solid color or in a pattern. The same fill options that you saw when you worked with pictures and text boxes are available for table cells.

1. Click inside a table to display the Table Tools.

2. Click the Design tab.

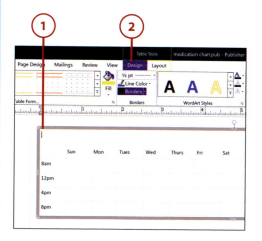

3. Select the cell or cells that you want to apply a fill to.

4. Click the Fill command button to open a palette of options.

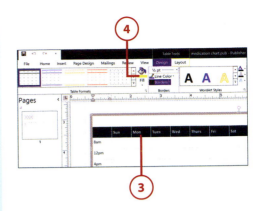

Select a color from either palette.

Choose from additional fill colors.

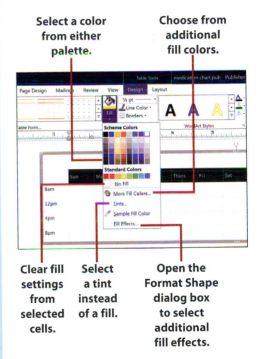

Clear fill settings from selected cells.

Select a tint instead of a fill.

Open the Format Shape dialog box to select additional fill effects.

Selecting Border Options

Initially, a table doesn't have a border. The thick border you see on-screen when you select it is a nonprintable border. It exists solely to delineate the dimensions of the table, as do the gridlines inside of the table. Those gray lines will not print either. You can easily add borders—using the border options.

1. Click inside a table to display the Table Tools.

2. Click the Design tab.

3. Select the cell(s) that you want to assign a border to.

4. Right-click in the selected cell(s) to display the QuickMenu.

5. Click Format Table.

Format Table Dialog Box

Although you can select from the Borders, Line Color, and Line Weight lists in the Borders group of the Design tab, it's more intuitive to use the Format Table dialog box. You can preview the settings before you actually apply them to the table.

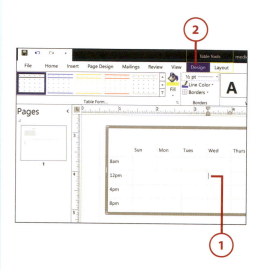

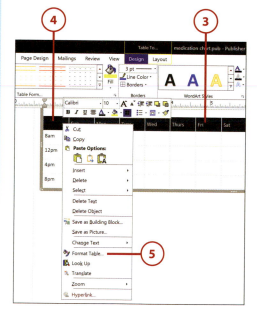

6. Click one of the preset buttons to assign a border to the cell(s).

7. Change the color of the border.

8. Click the spinner arrows to increase or decrease the line width.

9. Click OK when you are satisfied with the preview.

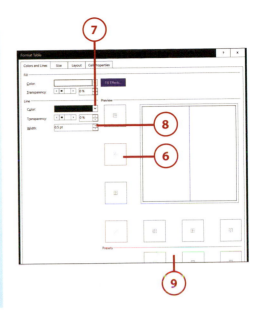

Importing Excel Spreadsheets and Graphs

If someone has already gone to the trouble to build a spreadsheet, and subsequently, some persuasive graphs, bring them right into Publisher! The beauty of software integration, and Microsoft Office suite integration in particular, is that you can import an Excel spreadsheet and graph seamlessly.

Importing a Spreadsheet

Sometimes, presenting the actual data is the most compelling way to deliver a report. Numbers don't lie, as is said, so a spreadsheet that shows how the numbers are related can be invaluable.

1. Click the Insert tab.

2. Click the Object command button to display the Insert Object dialog box.

3. Click Create from File to switch to browse features.

4. Click the Browse button to browse your system for the spreadsheet file.

5. When you locate the file, click Open.

6. Click OK to insert the file.

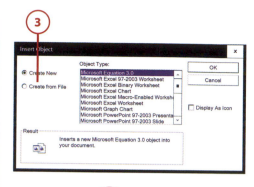

Importing Spreadsheets

Often, when you import a spread-sheet, you are left with a bunch of empty rows and columns. There is another method that is ideal for small spreadsheets: In Excel, select only the cells that you want to appear, and then press Ctrl+C to copy. Switch to Publisher, and then press Ctrl+V to paste the selected cells into the publication.

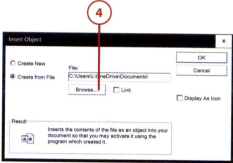

Paste Spreadsheet into Table

If you want to manipulate the rows and columns of data after you bring it into Publisher, you can paste a spreadsheet into a table. That table must already have the same number of rows and columns as the selected spreadsheet.

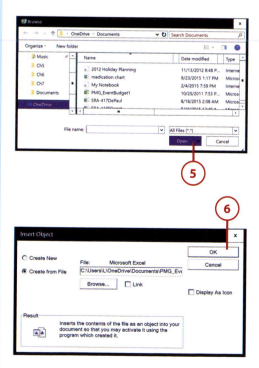

Link to a Spreadsheet

You may have noticed the Link check box in the Insert Object dialog box. This option creates a link to the spreadsheet, so any changes made in the spreadsheet will be reflected in the Publisher publication the next time it is opened.

Importing a Graph

Importing a graph into Publisher is a great way to illustrate your point and to capture your audience's attention. Nothing grabs them like a colorful graph, especially when it illustrates the data clearly and quickly.

As with almost everything in Publisher, there are a few ways to import a chart. Your time is valuable—let's go straight to the quickest and easiest way to import a chart into Publisher: copy and paste. Seriously.

1. In Excel, select the chart you want to import into Publisher.

2. On the Home tab, click Copy.

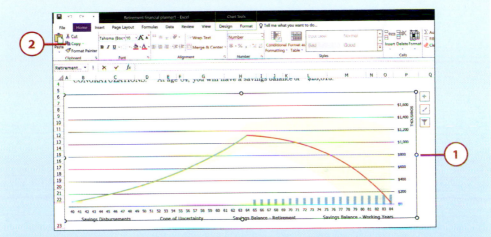

3. Back in Publisher, click Paste.

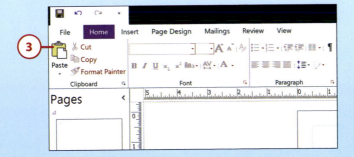

4. Select the imported chart to resize, move, or otherwise continue editing.

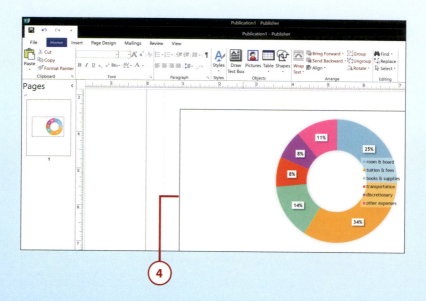

Headers and footers that contain dates, page numbers, revision numbers, and so on are ideal candidates for master pages.

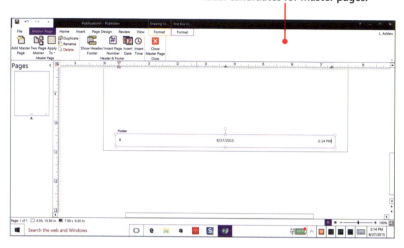

The Building Blocks Library has an impressive collection of bars, borders, and other accents.

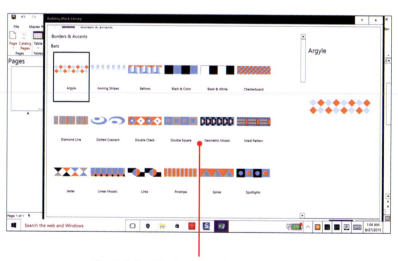

8

Working with Master Pages

Master pages are a little like templates. They contain the items that you want repeated on every page. For example, you can put a footer with the page number and date so that they appear on every page of the publication or a logo in the upper-left corner that you want to appear on every page. Anything that you find yourself repeating over and over—inserting an object, changing the formatting—may well be a good candidate for a master page.

Although you can let Publisher apply the contents of a master page to every page in your publication, you do have the option of associating a particular page with the None option, breaking the tie between the master page and that page. In this way, selected pages of a publication can be left out of the global formatting done by the master page.

You can create multiple master pages for more complex publications. Furthermore, you can create a two-page master page for publications that have facing pages, like a booklet, or brochure.

Creating a Master Page

Building a master page isn't that different from building a publication. You have all the formatting and tools available. The only difference is that everything you do is contained in one place, which makes editing much easier.

Master pages improve consistency in the appearance of your publications and improve productivity by reducing the amount of time you spend inserting objects and performing repetitive tasks.

1. From the Home tab, click the Page Design tab.

2. Click the Master Pages command button to open the list of options.

3. Click Edit Master Pages to switch to Master Page view.

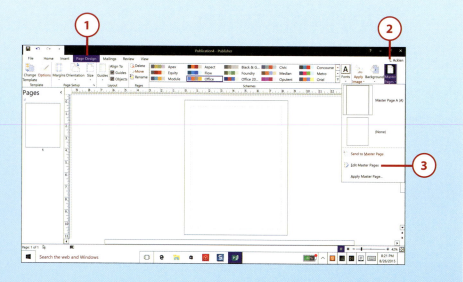

4. Click Show Header/Footer once to switch to the Header workspace.

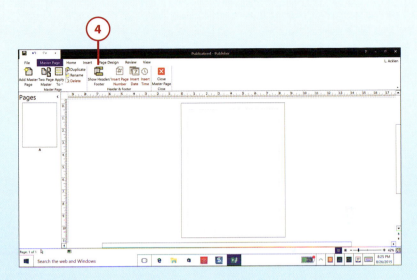

5. Click Show Header/Footer again to switch to the Footer workspace.

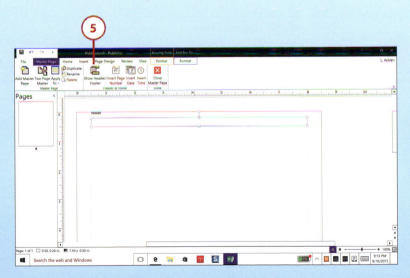

6. Click in the footer space.

7. Click the Insert Page Number command button.

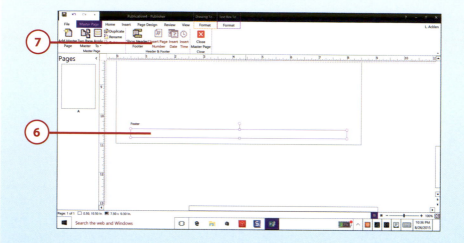

8. Press Tab to move to the center of the line.

9. Click the Insert Date command button.

10. Press Tab again to move to the right margin.

11. Click the Insert Time command button.

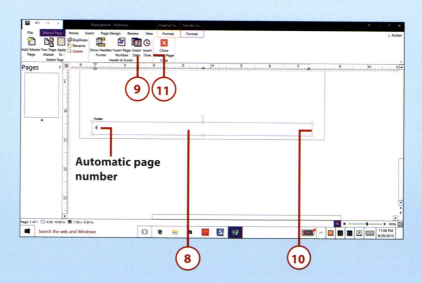

Automatic page number

12. Click Close Master Page when you finish.

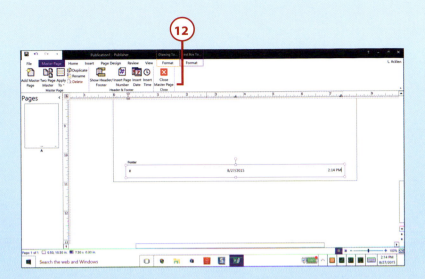

Two-Page Master

You can create a two-page master page for the publications that have facing pages. When you open the Master Page view, click the Two Page Master command button to change the default single page to a two-page master page. Then add the elements that you want to appear on the facing pages.

Applying Master Pages

In many cases, you will set up a master page that contains elements that you want to appear on every page. Publisher makes that incredibly simple because by default the master page is applied to all pages in the publication. So, you don't have to do a thing!

Still, it's a simple matter to create more than one master page and then selectively apply one or the other master to specific pages. The connection between the master page and a publication page can even be "broken," so none of the master pages are applied to it. Clearly, you have complete control over how the master pages are applied to the publication.

Applying a Master Page

There are two ways to apply a master page to your publication: either from the Publisher workspace or from the Master Page view.

1. Click on the page to which you want to apply a master page.

2. Click the Page Design tab.

3. Click the Master Pages command button.

4. Click Apply Master Page to display the Apply Master Page dialog box.

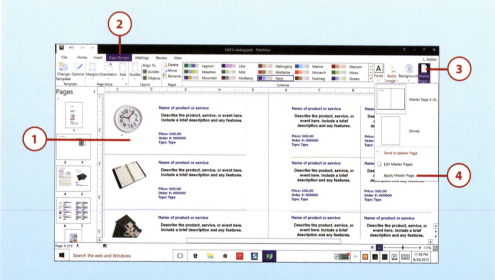

Use Apply To Command

You can also apply a master page from the Master Page view. Simply click the page where you want to apply a master page, and then click the Apply To command button. Click Apply to Current Page from the list of options.

5. If necessary, select the master page from this list.

6. Verify the Current Page(s) option is selected.

7. Click OK to apply the master page to the current page.

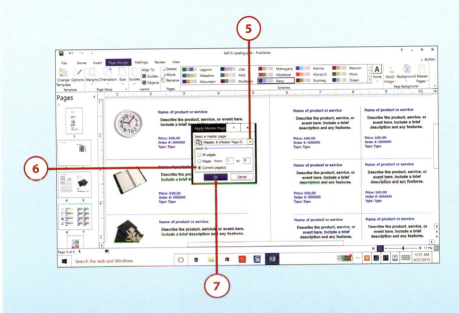

Rename a Master Page

Master pages are labeled with letters of the alphabet. The first master page is A, the second is B, and so forth. You can rename a master page in the Master Page view by clicking the Rename command button. In the Rename dialog box, make your changes, and then click OK.

Selecting None for the Master Page

When you need to un-apply (is that a word?) a master page, so that the elements in the master page are not placed on a specific page, you can break the connection. You simply choose (None) as the master page.

1.   Click the page from which you want to remove the master page.

2.   Click the Page Design tab.

3.   Click the Master Pages command button.

4.   Click the (None) option.

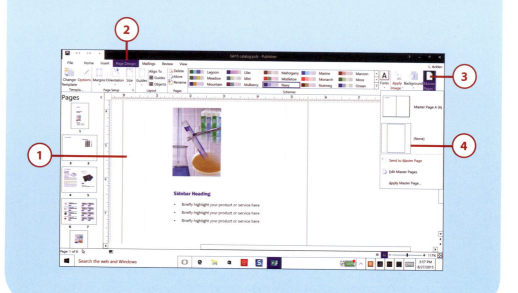

Editing Master Pages

Editing a master page is not much different from editing a publication. You do your work from the Master Page view rather than the Publisher workspace, but you have all the same tools available.

For this example, you need to edit the master page and add a banner. Using the Building Block Library, which contains items that let you assemble publications quickly and easily, you simply select from the impressive collection of built-in banners and bars.

1. Click the Page Design tab.

2. Click the Master Pages command button.

3. Click Edit Master Pages to switch to the Master Page view.

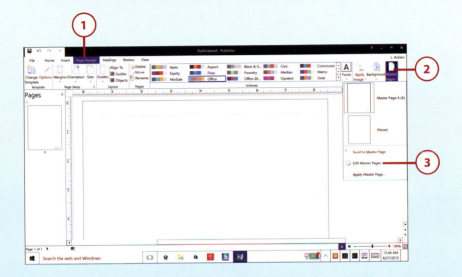

4. Click the Insert tab to gain access to those tools.

5. Click the Borders & Accents command button.

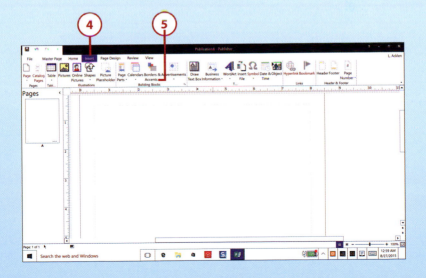

6. Scroll down to see the bars, emphasis, and frames.

7. Click More Borders and Accents to view the entire collection.

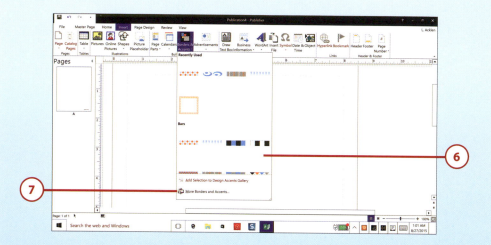

8. Scroll down through the Borders & Accents in the Building Block Library.

9. Double-click one of the borders/accents to insert it.

10. Click the Master Page tab to switch back to Master Page view.

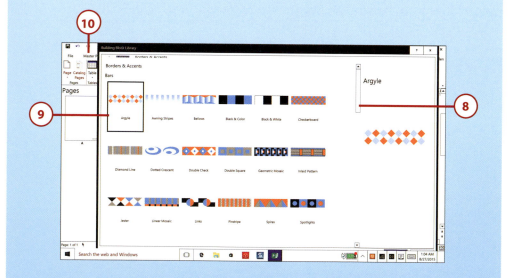

11.   Click the Close Master Page command button when you finish editing the master page.

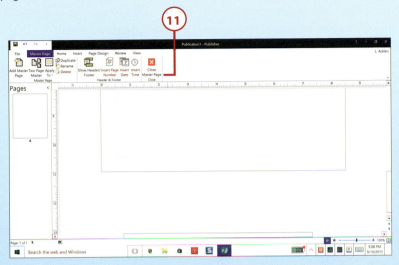

More Options

This exercise showed you how to insert a banner into a master page, which represents only one item that you can insert into a master page. The full gamut of tools are available on the Insert tab to include pictures, text boxes, shapes, WordArt, and tables to name a few. You also have all the tools on the Page Design tab.

>>>Go Further
ADD MORE MASTER PAGES

To add another master page to a publication, click the Page Design tab. Click the Master Pages command button, and then click Edit Master Pages. In the Master Pages view, click Add Master Page. When the New Master Page dialog box appears, either accept the single character page ID or change it to a different letter. If you like, edit the description. Either leave the two-page master check box enabled to create a two-page master, or disable it to create a single-page master. Click OK to create the additional master page.

Sending to the Master Page

One of the most popular aspects of the master page tool is your ability to deconstruct a publication and send objects to the master page, simplifying the publication by grouping together all the common elements in the master page. Editing those elements becomes much simpler, as does troubleshooting any issues you may have.

1. Select the item that you want to send to the master page.

2. Click the Page Design tab.

3. Click the Master Pages command button.

4. Click Send to Master Page.

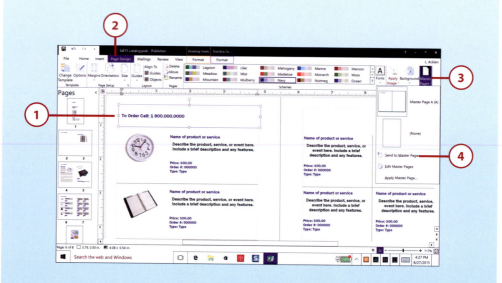

5. Click OK to continue working.

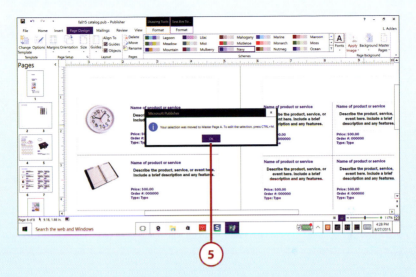

⑤

Publisher has a powerful mail merge feature that you can
use for mass mailings and other types of projects.

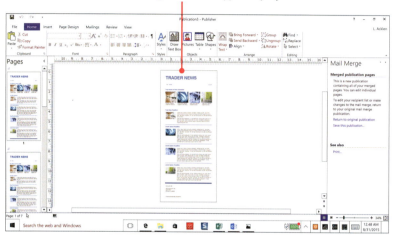

A variety of editing tasks can be done in the Mail
Merge Recipients dialog box.

9

Using Mail Merge to Distribute Publications

When you think of the merge feature, the first thing that comes to mind is a mail merge—generating personalized letters, postcards, newsletters, envelopes, and labels. What you may not realize right away is that the merge feature can be used to combine business data of any kind with publications of any kind. With a little imagination, you can use the merge feature to automate many, many tasks, not just bulk mailings.

A merge involves three basic steps: building a recipient list, preparing the publication, and merging the two together. After you establish the type of data that you want to combine with a publication, you then insert the markers that "stand in" for the business data in the publication. Those markers are replaced with the data when you combine the two.

So although these steps are for a typical mail merge, a recipient list could be an inventory list, a company directory, a price list, project schedule, or team roster, just to name a few.

Building a Recipient List

A typical recipient list consists of a name, company name, address (street, city, state, and ZIP code), phone number, and email address. The simplest method for maintaining contact information such as this is Outlook. For this reason, it is the first method discussed here.

The second method is to use an existing list. It's great to have this accessible—all you need is the location. Because the file may have originated in Access or Word, the screens may differ a bit from those you see here, where an Excel file was used.

Selecting Recipients from Outlook Contacts

Microsoft Outlook is one of the most powerful personal information managers on the market, and if that isn't reason enough to use it, consider the seamless integration between Outlook and the rest of the suite applications. When you have your contacts in Outlook, you can pull that information into any of the Office applications.

1. Open the publication that you want to use in the merge.

2. Click the Mailings tab.

3. Click the Select Recipients command button in the Start group.

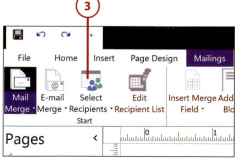

4. Click Choose from Outlook Contacts to open the Select Contacts dialog box.

5. Verify that your Contacts folder is being used.

6. Click OK to designate the Outlook Contacts folder as the source for the recipient list.

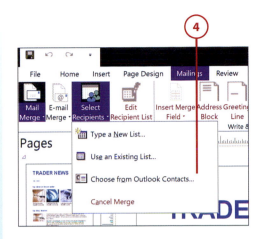

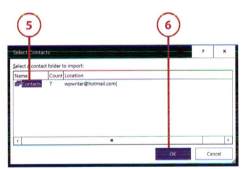

Using an Existing List

If you're lucky enough to have a list already provided to you, all you need to know is where it's located. This list might originate in Microsoft Access, the Microsoft Office Address Book, an Excel File, a Word document, the Publisher address books, or a text file. The important thing to remember is that the information is there—you just need to match it up to your publication.

1. Open the publication that you want to use in the merge.

2. Click the Mailings tab.

3. Click the Select Recipients command button in the Start group.

4. Click Use an Existing List.

5. Browse to the file and select it.

6. Click Open. The Select Table dialog box appears.

7. Verify that the selected table is the one you want to use.

8. Click OK to move to the Mail Merge Recipients dialog box.

More on Recipient Lists

For more information on working with recipient lists, see the "Editing Recipient Lists" section.

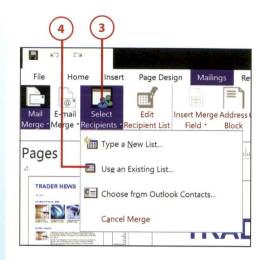

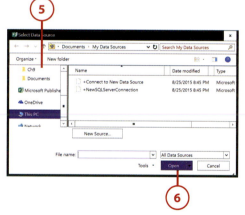

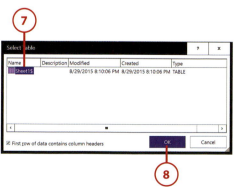

9. You can edit the table at this point, or wait until later.

10. Click OK to designate this table as the source for the recipient list.

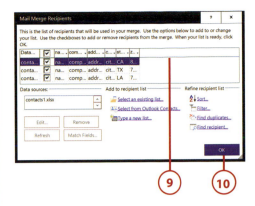

Creating a Fresh List

Creating a recipient list from scratch has some advantages. For one, you can decide exactly which fields you want to work with and customize the list so that entering the information is quick and easy. You may also find that for quick projects involving contact information from multiple sources, or one large source that requires significant filtering to isolate the right recipients, it's just simpler to type it in. And because you save the list, it's available the next time you need it.

1. Open the publication that you want to use in the merge.

2. Click the Mailings tab.

3. Click the Select Recipients command button in the Start group.

4. Click Type a New List. The New Address List dialog box opens.

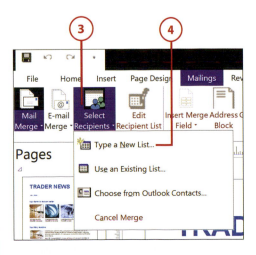

5. Click Customize Columns to open the Customize Address List dialog box.

6. Select a field that you will not use for this project.

7. Click Delete to remove it. Repeat to remove the extra fields.

8. Click Add and then type a name for the field to add a new field.

9. Select a field and click Rename to give it a new name.

10. Use these options to rearrange the list of fields.

11. Click OK when you finish.

Make It Fit

When you first see the New Address List dialog box, you will probably think that there is no way your information is going to fit in those tiny little boxes. Trust me—it will fit. You just won't see everything because the dialog box has limited real estate.

12. Type the name and address information. Press Tab to move to the next field.

13. Click OK to save this new list.

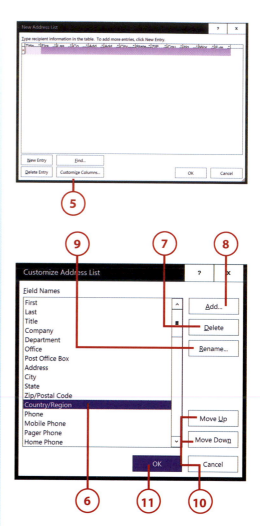

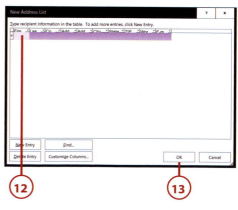

14. In the Save Address List dialog box, type a name for the file.

15. Click Save to save the address list file.

16. In the Mail Merge Recipients dialog box, click OK to designate this new address list as the source for the recipient.

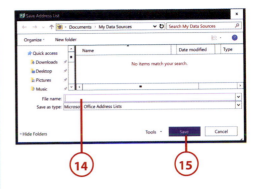

Change the Source

The source of the recipient list can always be changed. Simply click Select Recipients on the Mailings tab, and then choose the replacement source. Carefully read the messages that Publisher displays, and either confirm the replacement or leave it as-is.

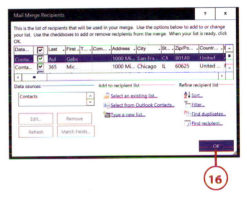

Editing Recipient Lists

Unless you just created a specific recipient for your project, you will likely want to pare down the contact list so that you have just the recipient list that you need. There are many ways to do this—you can select and deselect entries to add and remove people from the list.

You can also sort and filter the recipient list. For example, you can do a targeted mailing to just the companies located in San Jose, CA. Or you might want to single out all the clients who live in specific states. All this and more can be done by editing the lists.

Adding and Removing Recipients

In many cases, you will be starting with a large collection of contacts and need a method of narrowing down the list. For small- to medium-sized lists, you can remove recipients from the list by simply disabling the check box next to each name. If you change your mind, enable the check box to add them back in.

1. Open the publication that you want to use in the merge.

2. Click the Mailings tab.

3. Click the Edit Recipient List command button in the Start group.

4. Scroll down through the list of contacts.

5. Enable/disable the check boxes to remove and add back in recipients from the merge.

6. Click OK when you finish.

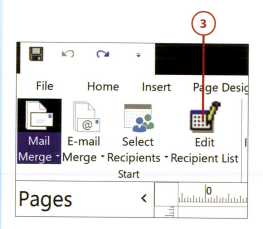

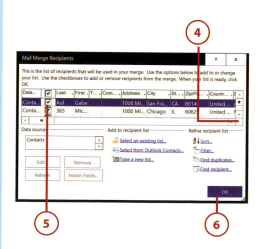

Filtering the Recipient List

Larger lists are managed more easily with filtering and sorting tools. What's the difference, you ask? Filtering a list actually pares it down, removing irrelevant records from view. Sorting rearranges the list without removing any of the records from view.

1. Open the publication that you want to use in the merge.

2. Click the Mailings tab.

3. Click the Edit Recipient List command button to display the Mail Merge Recipients dialog box.

4. Click Filter to display the Filter and Sort dialog box.

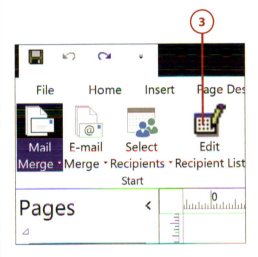

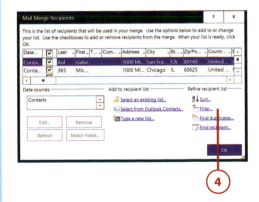

5. Click the Field down arrow to open the list of fields.

6. Select the field you want to filter by.

7. Click the Comparison down arrow to open a list of comparisons.

8. Select the type of comparison you want to perform.

9. Type the value for the comparison.

10. Add additional comparisons by selecting AND or OR here.

11. Click OK when you finish. Publisher will filter the recipients.

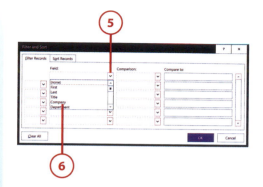

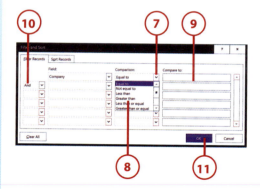

Find a Recipient

You can quickly locate a particular entry in a recipient list. In the Mail Merge Recipients dialog box, click Find Recipient to open the Find Entry dialog box. Type the name or other identifying piece of information in the Find box; then click Find Next.

Clear Filters

When you are ready to restore the recipient list to its original state, or if you just want to start over so that you can set up a different set of filters, click Clear All in the Filter and Sort dialog box to reset everything.

Sorting the Recipient List

When you sort a list, you rearrange it, so it's easier to work with. Sorting by last name and then first name quickly shows you duplicates, for example. Sorting by ZIP code allows you to zero in on those specific regions. Sorting does not hide any recipients from view, the way filtering does.

1. Open the publication that you want to use in the merge.

2. Click the Mailings tab.

3. Click the Edit Recipient List command button to open the Mail Merge Recipients dialog box.

4. Click Sort to display the Filter and Sort dialog box.

5. Click the Sort by down arrow to open the list of fields.

6. Select the field you want to sort by.

7. Choose between an ascending and descending sort.

8. Continue selecting additional sort fields if necessary.

9. Click OK to sort the recipient list.

Clear Sorts

When you are ready to restore your recipient list to its original state, or if you simply want to start over so that you can create a different type of sort, click Clear All in the Filter and Sort dialog box to start fresh.

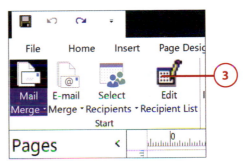

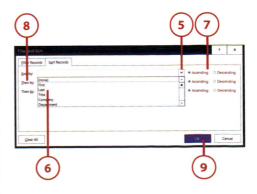

Setting Up the Publication Document

An existing publication can be turned into a merge document in just seconds. You will insert merge fields that act as markers in the publication. They "stand in" for the actual information that will be inserted during the merge. As such, you can place your punctuation around these fields. Placing a merge field on a line by itself ensures that the information has plenty of space.

Merge fields are easy to understand. Depending on the source for your recipient list, you will be inserting codes like <<First>> for first name, <<Last >> for last name, and so on. Surrounding the field with << and >> identifies that information as a merge field and delineates it from the rest of the text.

1. With a publication that has a recipient list already associated with it open in Publisher, click the Mailings tab.

2. Position the insertion point where you want to insert a field.

3. Click the Insert Merge Field command button.

4. Click the field that you want to insert. Publisher inserts it between "<<" and ">>".

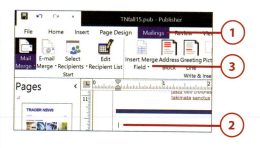

Tidying Up

All the punctuation and formatting happens in the publication. The recipient list is strictly data. So as you add merge fields in a publication, add the formatting, punctuation, and spacing as you go.

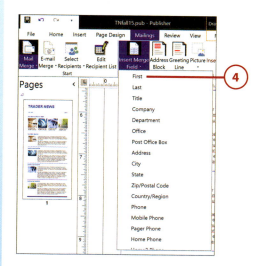

5. Insert a space or other punctuation.

6. Insert the next field.

7. Continue adding fields to complete the address block.

8. Save your work (frequently).

Address Book

The Address Block command button on the Mailings tab opens the Insert Address Block dialog box, where you can specify *exactly* how you want an address to appear. There are some fancy options that allow you to choose from a comprehensive list of formats for the recipient's name and that help you work with country/regions in the address block.

Greeting Line

The Greeting Line command button on the Mailings tab opens the Insert Greeting Line dialog box, where you can specify *exactly* how you want the salutation to appear. There is also a list of generic greetings, so if merge finds an invalid recipient name, Publisher will insert an appropriate greeting line.

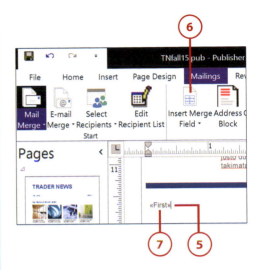

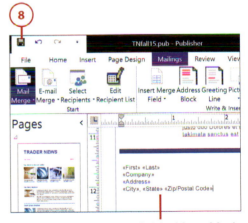

A completed merge field address block

Merge the List with the Publication

Now that you have a recipient list ready and the publication has been prepared, you are ready to merge the two together. When the merge takes place, the merge fields are matched with the fields in the recipient list, and the recipient information is pulled in to replace the merge fields.

At the end of the merge, you have a series of merged publications. If you plan to print these publications so that you can deliver them by hand or snail mail, you can do this easily. You can also save the merge results; although, this is actually saving the same information twice. Remember, you can always merge the two together whenever you need the merged publications again.

1. With a publication that has a recipient list already associated with it open in Publisher, click the Mailings tab.

2. Click the Finish & Merge command button.

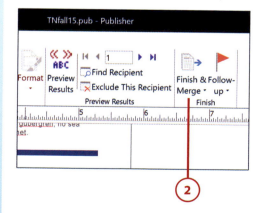

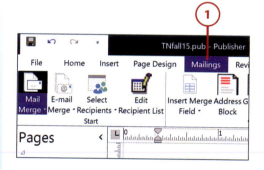

3. Click Merge to New Publication.

4. Click the Close button to clear the Mail Merge pane.

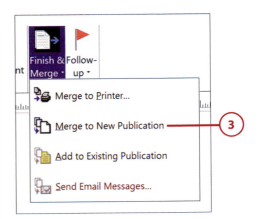

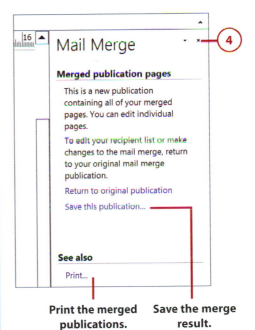

Print the merged publications.   **Save the merge result.**

>>>*Go Further*

FIXING MERGE PROBLEMS

If the results of the merge aren't quite what you thought they would be, it's probably a simple fix. Scan through the merged publications and see if you can detect a pattern. Is the state where the city should be? Are all the last names missing, or just the last several? If the same problem happens again and again, go to the publication first. Make sure you have the merge fields in the right place. If you need to replace a field, delete the old one and reinsert a new one. Save your changes and try the merge again. Now, if the problem occurs in just two or three entries, take a look at the recipient list. Make sure the city isn't actually in the State field. Zero in on those recipients whose addresses were mixed up. Make your corrections, save the changes, and retry the merge.

Using the Merge Wizards

Publisher includes two wizards to walk you step-by-step through the process: the Mail Merge Wizard and the Email Merge Wizard. Publisher's Mail Merge Wizard takes you by the hand and leads you through the three-step process to setting up a mail merge with a publication. The Email Merge Wizard takes you through essentially the same steps with small adjustments for emailing, rather than mailing.

There is more information on each of the steps in the previous sections of this chapter. You can either go through the steps "manually" as you've learned thus far, or you can use this wizard to keep you on track.

Using the Mail Merge Wizard

Remember when you merge your publication with a recipient list, you don't have to save the results because you can always merge the two files together again. The only reason you might want to save the merged publications is if you want to work on it later, perhaps to polish a few things.

1. Click the Mailings tab.

2. Click the Mail Merge command button in the Start group.

3. Click Step-by-Step Mail Merge Wizard.

4. Read the information that Publisher shows you initially.

5. Scroll down to select one of the recipient list options.

6. For this example, enable the Select from Outlook Contacts option.

More on Recipients

For more information on using an existing recipient list, or typing a new list, see the earlier "Building a Recipient List" section.

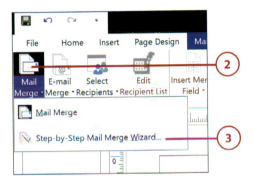

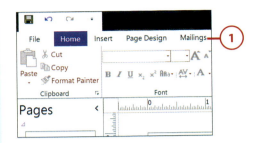

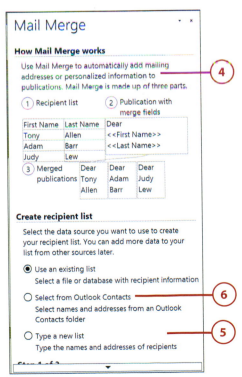

7. Click Next: Create or connect to a recipient list.

8. Verify the correct profile (most likely Outlook).

9. Click OK. The Select Contact dialog box appears.

10. Verify that you want to pull from the Contacts folder.

11. Click OK. The Mail Merge Recipients dialog box appears.

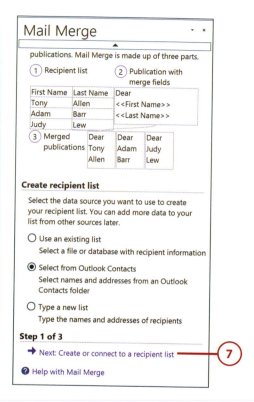

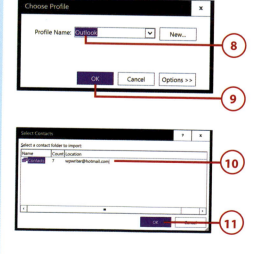

12. Make any necessary changes to the recipient list.

13. Click OK. Now the Mail Merge Wizard is prompting you for Step 2.

14. Drag and drop these pieces of the recipient information into your publication.

15. Click Address fields to open the Insert Address Field dialog box.

More Information

For more information on inserting address blocks and greeting lines, see the section "Setting Up the Publication Document."

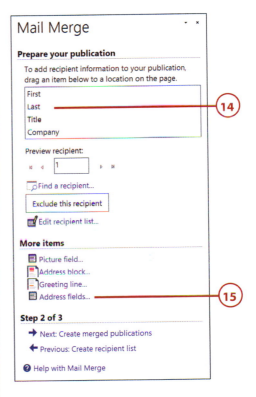

16. Click an address field.

17. Click Insert to place it in your publication.

18. Repeat steps 16 and 17 to insert all the fields you need, and then click Cancel to clear the dialog box.

19. Click Next: Create merged publications.

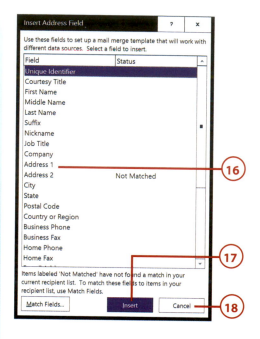

20. Click Merge to a new publication.

21. Choose from one of these options to continue working with the merged publications.

22. Close the Mail Merge pane when you are done.

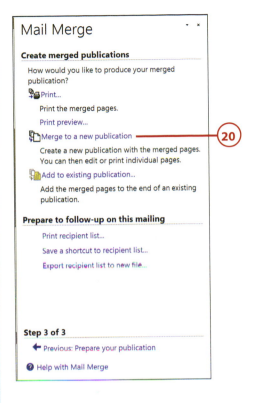

Using the Email Merge Wizard

As you'll see, the Email Merge Wizard is designed to step you through the process of putting together a merge that is emailed to recipients, rather than hand-delivered or snail-mailed. The steps differ slightly to accommodate email addresses rather than street addresses.

1. Click the Mailings tab.

2. Click the E-mail Merge command button in the Start group.

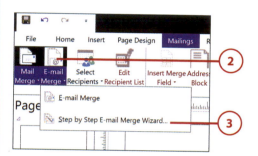

3. Click Step-by-Step E-mail Merge Wizard.

4. Read the information that Publisher shows you initially.

5. Select one of the recipient list options.

6. For this example, enable the Select from Outlook Contacts option.

More on Recipient Lists

For more information on using an existing recipient list, or typing a new list, see the previous "Building a Recipient List" section.

Why Outlook?

Outlook is used as the source for the recipient list here because of the superior integration with Publisher. If your recipient list is in another format, such as an Excel file or a Word document, you can use that as a recipient list with no problem.

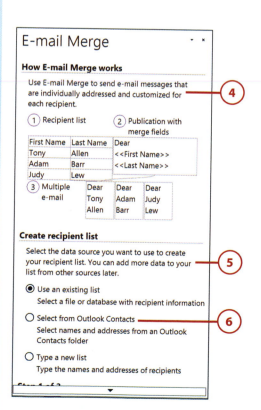

7. Click Next: Create or connect to a recipient list.

8. Verify the correct profile (in this example, an Outlook profile).

9. Click OK. The Select Contact dialog box appears.

10. Verify that you want to pull from the Contacts folder.

11. Click OK. The Mail Merge Recipients dialog box appears.

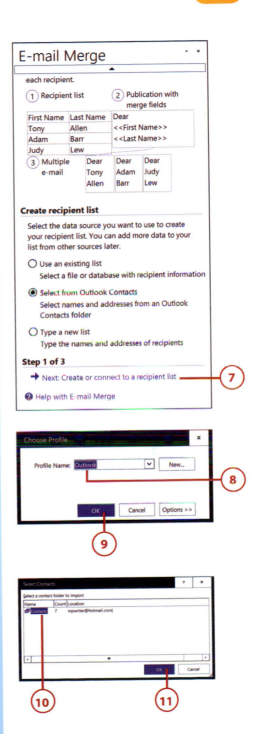

12. Make any necessary changes to the recipient list.

13. Click OK. The E-mail Merge Wizard is ready for you to prepare the publication.

14. Drag and drop pieces of the recipient information into your publication.

15. Scroll down through the list to continue adding all the fields you need.

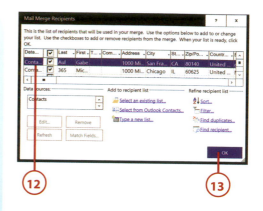

More Information

For more information on inserting address blocks and greeting lines, see the "Setting Up the Publication Document" section.

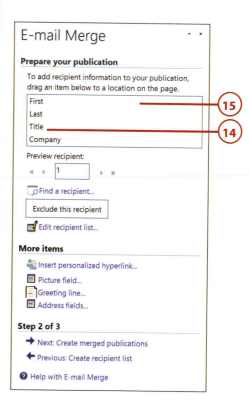

16. Click Next: Create merged publications.

17. Click E-mail preview so you can take a look.

E-mail Merge

Prepare your publication

To add recipient information to your publication, drag an item below to a location on the page.

> Address
> City
> State
> Zip/Postal Code

Preview recipient:

⊲⊲ ◁ 1 ▷ ▷▷

🔍Find a recipient...

Exclude this recipient

📝 Edit recipient list...

More items

👥 Insert personalized hyperlink...

🖼 Picture field...

📄 Greeting line...

🖼 Address fields...

Step 2 of 3

➡ Next: Create merged publications

⬅ Previous: Create recipient list

❷ Help with E-mail Merge

E-mail Merge

Select E-mail Merge Output

Your e-mail messages are ready to send.

📧 Send e-mail...

Select an e-mail account and send your publication as customized e-mail messages.

E-mail preview...

1 potential issue(s) found with this e-mail. Use the Design Checker to resolve these issues.

Design Checker...

Prepare to follow-up on this mailing

Print recipient list...

Save a shortcut to recipient list...

Export recipient list to new file...

Step 3 of 3

⬅ Previous: Prepare your publication

❷ Help with E-mail Merge

18. Close the browser window when you finish.

19. Close the E-mail Merge pane when you are done.

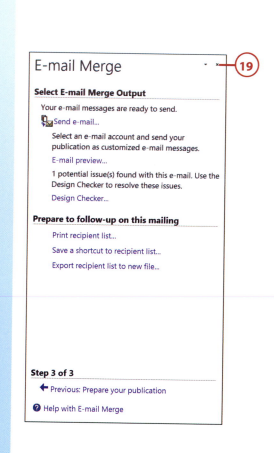

Publisher flags potential problems in the Design Checker pane. You can take care of each issue, one-by-one until the list is empty.

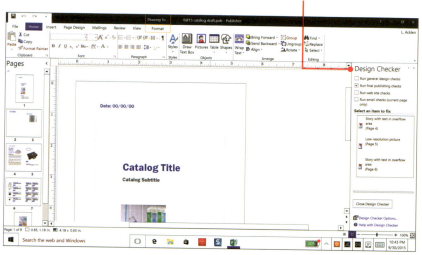

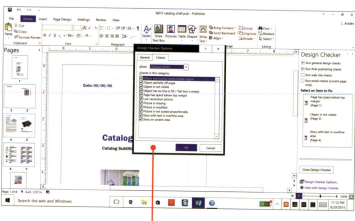

Using the Design Checker Options dialog box, you can control all aspects of the check.

Using the Design Checker

The Design Checker is a wonderful built-in mistake preventer. For those of us who fumble around a bit, it's great to know that we can run the Design Checker before we let *anyone* else see our publication. It checks the publication for design and layout problems and then offers solutions to fix them.

There are four different types of checks: general design, commercial printing, web site, and e-mail. Each type is designed to work with a specific type of publication. It is strongly recommended that you run Design Checker before you print, package it for a commercial printer, publish to the web, or after you convert a publication.

Checking the Publication for Problems

The Design Checker command button is located in the Backstage area. When you start the Design Checker, a new pane appears on the right. You use the options on the Design Checker pane to control the check and to fix problems.

When the Design Checker pane is open, it dynamically updates the list of potential problems as they occur, and as you fix them. Sometimes, fixing one problem leads to another. Take a deep breath and tackle each problem, one at a time. That list will dwindle down into nothing in just minutes.

Running Your First Design Check

As previously mentioned, you can run four different types of checks on your publication, depending on the intended purpose. Before going into detail on each type of check, let's run through a basic general design check to give you an idea of how the process works.

1. Click the File tab to switch to the Backstage area.

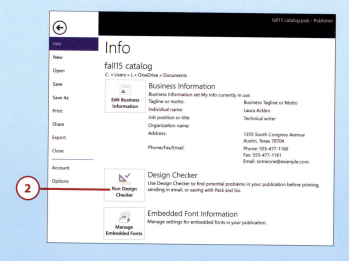

2. Click the Run Design Checker button to display the Design Checker pane in the publication window.

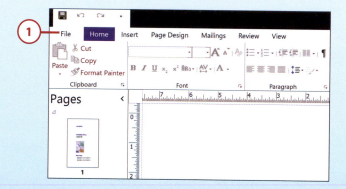

3. Select the first potential problem. Publisher moves to that page and displays the object.

Design Checker pane

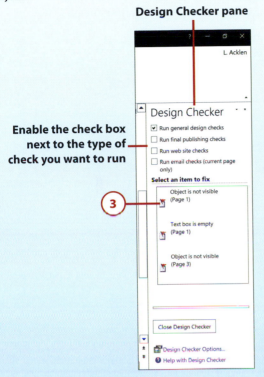

Enable the check box next to the type of check you want to run

4. Point to the right side of the problem box until you see an arrow bar.

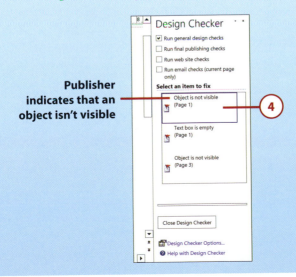

Publisher indicates that an object isn't visible

5. Click the arrow bar to display other options.

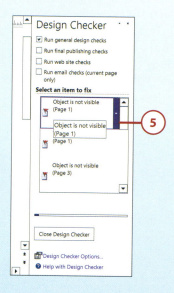

6. Click Explain to display the Publisher 2016 Help window.

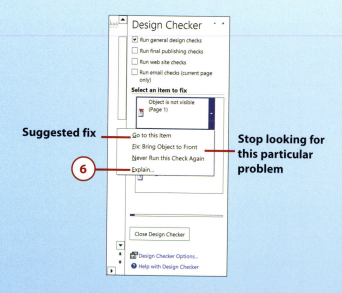

Suggested fix

Stop looking for this particular problem

7. Type a search word or phrase into the Search box.

8. Click the magnifying glass to start the search.

9. Click the Using the Design Checker in Publisher help topic for more information.

10. Close the Help window when you finish reading.

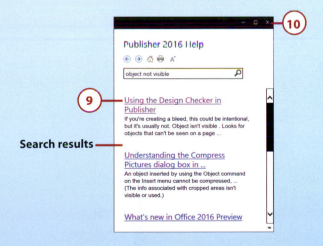

11. Display the arrow bar again.

12. Click Fix: Bring Object to Front.

13. Select the object and move it aside. Chances are there is another object underneath.

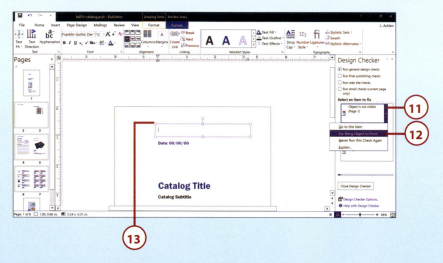

14. Select the extra object and delete it. After a few seconds, that problem no longer appears in the list.

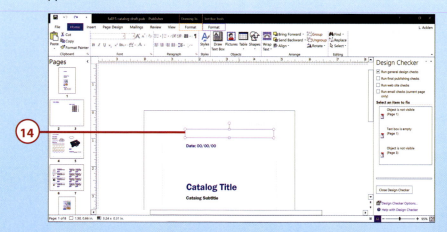

15. Select the next potential problem.

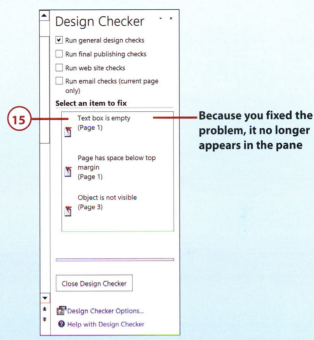

Because you fixed the problem, it no longer appears in the pane

16. Delete the empty text box.

17. Repeat these steps until you have taken care of the potential problems.

18. Click Close Design Checker when you finish.

Publisher selects the empty text box

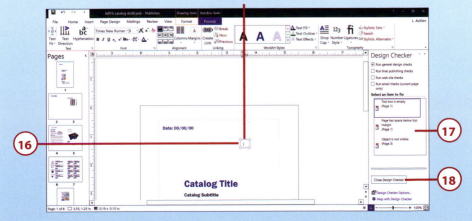

>>>*Go Further*
SAVING ALL THOSE CORRECTIONS

It's always a good idea to save your work (often), but with Design Checker, it's a necessity. You've just corrected some potential problems, some of them "deal breakers." What good would all that effort be if you didn't save your changes? I like the shortcut key Alt+F, S. I've made it a habit to press that key combination whenever I stop to gather my thoughts.

Running a General Check

A General Design check is just what it sounds like—it scans the document for common design problems, such as the empty text box and overlapping objects that you saw earlier. These may not cause formatting problems. That's why I call them "potential" problems. If you have trouble figuring out what a problem is, and your publication looks fine when you print it, you may opt to skip the problem.

1. Click the File tab to switch to the Backstage area.

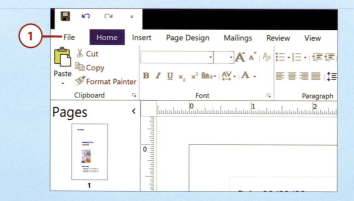

2. Click the Run Design Checker button to display the Design Checker pane in the publication window.

3. Verify that the Run general design checks check box is enabled.

4. Select the first potential problem in the Design Checker pane.

5. Continue working through the list of problems.

6. Click the Close Design Checker button when you finish.

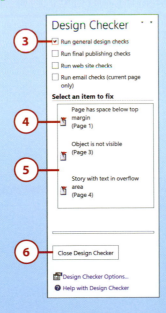

Running a Commercial Printing Check

The final publishing checks are specifically designed to catch mistakes that can cause problems when you have a publication professionally printed. Common issues include setting a publication to print in RGB colors, low-resolution pictures, missing pictures, and so on. This type of mistake can be expensive if caught after a large print run.

1. Click the File tab to switch to the Backstage area.

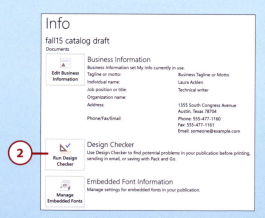

2. Click the Run Design Checker button to display the Design Checker pane in the publication window.

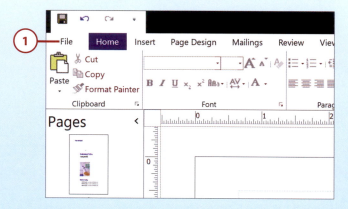

3. Enable the Run final publishing checks check box.

4. Select the first potential problem in the Design Checker pane.

5. Continue working through the list of problems.

6. Click the Close Design Checker button when you finish.

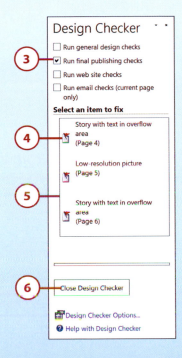

Run Other Checks

You can enable more than one type of check in the Design Checker pane. For example, you may want to run all the general design checks as well as e-mail checks. Note also that e-mail checks are run only on the current page.

Running a Web Site Check

Potential problems with web pages are the focus of the Run Web Site Checks option. The check looks for pictures without alternative text, pages that can't be reached from the first page, and pages that don't have a link to leave the page.

1. Click the File tab to switch to the Backstage area.

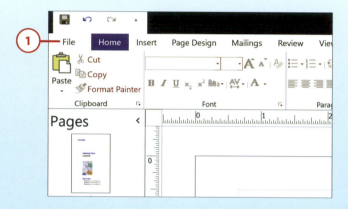

2. Click the Run Design Checker button to display the Design Checker pane in the publication window.

3. Enable the Run web site checks check box.

4. Select the first potential problem in the Design Checker pane.

5. Continue working through the list of problems.

6. Click the Close Design Checker button when you finish.

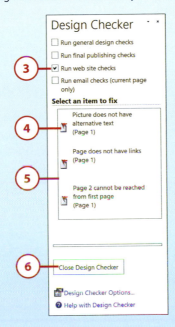

Running an Email Check

The Email checks option looks for potential problems with creating publications that are destined for email messages. This check finds issues with objects that overlap text boxes, objects containing text that may have been accidentally rotated, text boxes with vertical text, and a handful more.

1. Click the File tab to switch to the Backstage area.

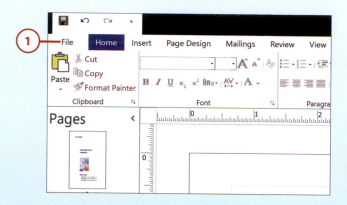

2. Click the Run Design Checker button to display the Design Checker pane in the publication window.

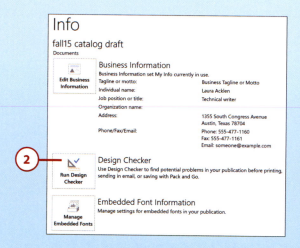

3. Enable the Run email checks (current page only) check box.

4. Select the first potential problem in the Design Checker pane.

5. Continue working through the list of problems.

6. Click the Close Design Checker button when you finish.

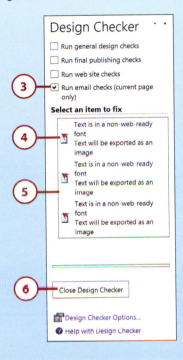

Setting Design Checker Options

The Design Checker Options dialog box is the command center: the place where you control exactly what Publisher looks for in each of the four checks previously described. You can also customize how the task pane displays the problems that it finds, and set which pages you want the Design Checker to set.

Selecting Options on the General Tab

The General tab has just a couple sections: Display Options and Page Range. The Sort by list enables you to choose how you want the potential problems arranged: by page number, by description, or by status.

The default is to remove the items that are fixed so that eventually you are left with an empty list. If you collaborate with others on the publication, you may want to leave those on the list. Simply disable the Remove fixed items check box.

The Page Range section enables you to limit the check to the current page, versus all the pages. You can also enable or disable the option to check master page(s).

1. Click the File tab to switch to the Backstage area.

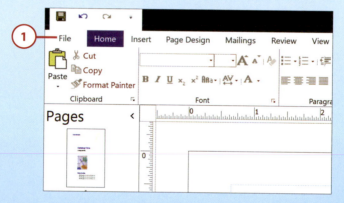

2. Click the Run Design Checker button to display the Design Checker pane in the publication window.

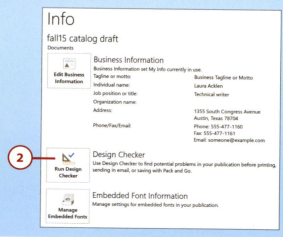

3. Click Design Checker Options to display the Design Checker Options dialog box.

4. On the General tab, click the Sort by arrow to open the list of options.

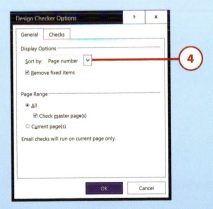

5. If you like, choose another option to rearrange the list.

6. Disable the Remove fixed items check box if you would prefer to leave fixed problems in the list.

7. If you prefer not to check master pages, disable the Check master page(s) check box.

8. Enable the Current page(s) option if you want to check only the current page, or the currently selected pages.

9. Click OK if you want to save your changes, or click Cancel to clear the dialog box.

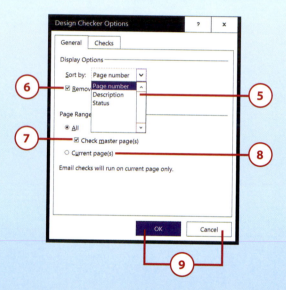

Enabling/Disabling Checks on the Checks Tab

For extremely complex publications, you can customize the way Design Checker works by enabling and disabling the checks for each category on the Checks tab. Is it necessary for a routine publication? Not at all. However, if you move past the same potential problem over and over, maybe you should disable that check.

1. Click the File tab to switch to the Backstage area.

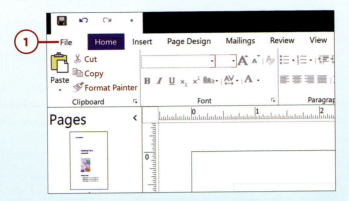

2. Click the Run Design Checker button to display the Design Checker pane in the publication window.

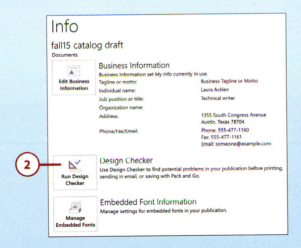

3. Click Design Checker Options to display the Design Checker Options dialog box.

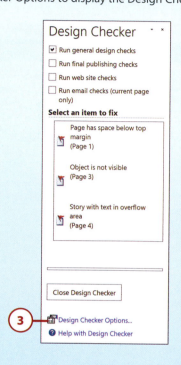

4. Click the Checks tab.

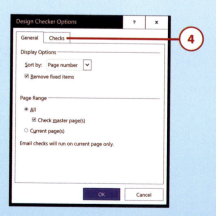

5.   Click the Show arrow to open the list of checks you can control.

6.   Select one of the other checks to narrow down the list to just those options.

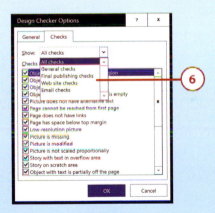

7. Disable items in the list by removing the check marks.

8. Click OK when you finish.

Check All

Selecting All Checks in the Show list displays the checks performed for all of the categories.

Exploring the General Checks Options

Narrowing down the list of checks that are done makes it much easier to work with only those options that you are using. For example, it doesn't make sense to scroll past options for website checks if you aren't preparing your publication for the web.

Specifically, the checks performed during a General Checks run are as follows.

This	Does This
Object encroaches non-printable region	Publisher warns you when an object is in the unprintable region of your printer (usually ¼" away from the edges).
Object partially off page	Publisher warns you when an object won't print completely because it's off the page. If you are going for a bleed effect, this may be intentional.
Object isn't visible	Publisher looks for objects that, for one reason or another, aren't visible on the page.

Object doesn't have a line or fill/Text box is empty	Publisher looks for objects that do not have opaque attributes. This could be an AutoShape with no lines/fill or an empty text box.
Object has transparency	Publisher looks for objects with a transparent color applied to them. Objects with transparent colors print with unpredictable results on some PostScript/PCL printers.
Page has space below the top margin	Publisher looks for pages where no objects touches, or is above, the top margin.
Low-resolution picture	Publisher is on the lookout for pictures with a resolution of less than 96 dpi. This is important for two reasons: one, printing to a high-resolution printer/imagesetter requires high-resolution pictures; and two, because 96 dpi is the resolution that is recommended for PDF and XPS files.
Picture is missing	Publisher looks for broken links to picture files that may have been deleted or moved.
Picture is modified	Publisher checks to make sure that all linked pictures have been updated.
Picture isn't scaled proportionately	Publisher can tell if a picture has been sized in one dimension more than the others and will tell you that the picture is disproportionate.
Story with text in overflow	Publisher looks for a text box or AutoShape that has part of the story that isn't visible because it's in overflow.
Story on scratch area	Publisher checks linked text boxes and AutoShapes to make sure that there isn't a part of the story on the scratch area.
Text has transparent colors	Publisher scans for text with transparent colors because those colors print unpredictably on PostScript and PCL printers.
Text has transparent effects	Publisher scans for text with transparent effects applied because those effects will print unpredictably on PostScript/PCL printers.

It's Transparent

If you want to use transparent colors or effects, it's best to save the publication in PDF or XPS. You can also opt to print to XPS Enhanced Printer.

Exploring the Final Publishing Checks Options

Selecting the Final Publishing Checks in the Show list narrows the list of checks to just those for commercial printing.

The checks performed during a Final Publishing Checks run are as follows.

This	Does That
More than two spot colors	Publisher zeros in on the use of more than two spot colors if a publication is configured to be printed "spot-color" or "process-color and spot-color."
Unused spot colors	Publisher goes through and locates a stray spot-color ink if there is one in the ink list, but it wasn't used in the publication. This check runs only if you set up the publication's Color Model to "spot-color" or "process-color and spot-color."
Publication is in RGB mode	Publisher looks for a print mismatch. If you have your publication set to print in RGB colors but everything else is set up for commercial printing, you will be warned.
Object has transparency	Publisher scans for objects that have a transparent color applied to them. Remember, transparent colors print strangely on PostScript/PCL printers.
Low-resolution picture	Publisher is on the lookout for pictures with a resolution of less than 96 dpi. This is important for two reasons: one, printing to a high-resolution printer/imagesetter requires high-resolution pictures; and two, because 96 dpi is the resolution that is recommended for PDF and XPS files.
Story with text in overflow	Publisher looks for a text box or AutoShape that has part of the story that isn't visible because it's in overflow.
Story on scratch area	Publisher checks linked text boxes and AutoShapes to make sure that there isn't a part of the story on the scratch area.
Text has transparent colors	Publisher scans for text with transparent colors since those colors print strangely on PostScript and PCL printers.
Text has transparent effects	Publisher scans for text with transparent effects applied because those effects print strangely on PostScript/PCL printers.

It's Transparent

If you want to use transparent colors or effects, it's best to save the publication in PDF or XPS. You can also opt to print to XPS Enhanced Printer.

Exploring the Web Site Checks Options

The three web site checks are self-explanatory.

This	Does That
Picture doesn't have alternative text	Publisher identifies pictures that are not set up with alternative text (for accessibility).
Page can't be reached from first page	Publisher checks for pages that can't be found either by a combination of links that begin from a link on the first (home) page of the web site.
Page doesn't have links	Publisher looks for pages that don't have a link to leave the page. For example, a Back or Previous button.

Exploring the Email Checks Options

Now consider the Email Checks options. Publisher runs through the publication looking for issues related to e-mailing the publication. The options for Email checks are as follows.

This	Does That
Object with text is partially off the page	Publisher locates objects containing text that runs off the publication page.
HTML fragment is partially off the page	Publisher finds stray HTML code fragments that might extend off the page.
Object is overlapping text	Publisher looks for any object that is placed on top of a text box.
Object with text is rotated	Publisher checks for objects that contain text and have been rotated.
Shape with text has a hyperlink on the shape	Publisher locates any shape with a hyperlink on top of it.
Text is vertical	Publisher looks for text boxes that contain vertically rotated text.
Text is too big to fit in the frame	Publisher scans for text boxes that have too much text to fit in the frame.
Text is in a nonweb-ready font	Publisher scans for text that is formatted in a font that isn't ready for web prime time.
Text is in a diagonal table cell	Publisher finds text that is inside a diagonal table cell.
Table borders are less than .75 pts	Publisher flags table borders of less than .75pts thick.
Text has hyphenation	Publisher scans for hyphens in the text.
Text box with borders has zero margins	Publisher scans for text boxes with a margin set to zero.
Hyperlink links to another page in this publication	Publisher locates hyperlinks on a web page that link to another page in the same publication.

Publisher's AutoCorrect tool makes it easy for you to correct typos and spelling mistakes as you work.

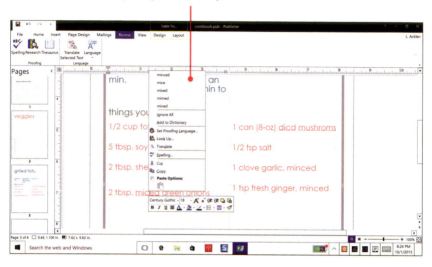

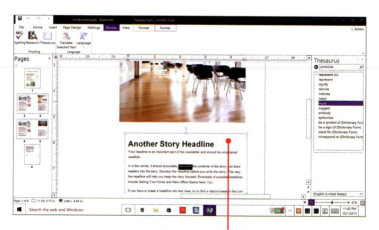

The Thesaurus can help you improve the readability and variety of your publications.

Proofing Tools

Spell checkers have become so common, you probably can't think of a single program or app that doesn't have one. We all know and love the autocorrect on our phones—turning our messages into gobbledygook for us. Thankfully, Publishers proofing tools are much less intrusive.

When you are ready, it's always a good idea to do a quick run-through with the speller checker, just to make sure there are no typos or goofy mistakes. In addition, don't let the word "thesaurus" scare you—Publisher's built-in thesaurus is super easy to use. When you use the same word or phrase repeatedly, try it and see if you can get inspired.

Working with AutoCorrect

Even the most thoroughly researched, professionally presented publication can lose credibility with a few spelling errors. Back in the day when most executives had assistants, they didn't have to worry about details like spelling and punctuation. Now we all take care of our own correspondence and publications, so it is important to take a few minutes to run a spell check.

Publisher has two tools to catch spelling errors: AutoCorrect and Spelling. AutoCorrect prompts you to correct spelling errors and typos as you type. Some people don't like the interruption and turn off AutoCorrect and run spell check later.

Correcting Errors with AutoCorrect

AutoCorrect is configured to run automatically when you install Office. AutoCorrect compares the words in your document with words in the main dictionary. If it finds a mismatch, AutoCorrect underlines the word with red dotted lines. Right-clicking the word brings up a QuickMenu with suggestions and additional commands.

1. Right-click an underlined word to display the AutoCorrect QuickMenu.

Misspelled words

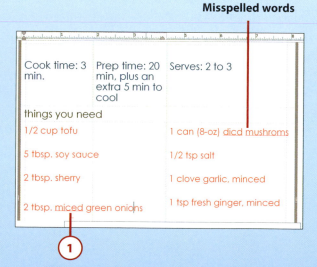

Cook time: 3 min.   Prep time: 20 min, plus an extra 5 min to cool   Serves: 2 to 3

things you need

1/2 cup tofu

5 tbsp. soy sauce

2 tbsp. sherry

2 tbsp. miced green onions

1 can (8-oz) dicd mushroms

1/2 tsp salt

1 clove garlic, minced

1 tsp fresh ginger, minced

1

2. Click the correctly spelled word at the top of the list.

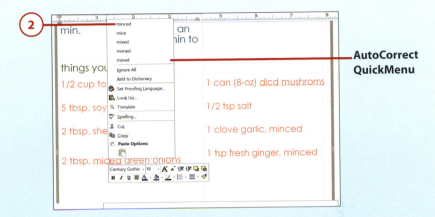

AutoCorrect QuickMenu

3. Right-click the other misspelled words/typos and correct them.

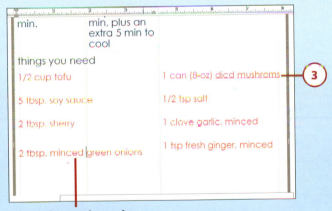

Publisher replaces the misspelled word with the correctly spelled word you selected.

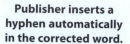

Publisher inserts a hyphen automatically in the corrected word.

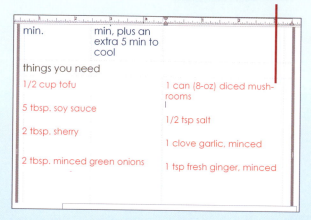

Adding Words to the Dictionary from AutoCorrect

When you work on your content and correcting typos and mistakes as you go with AutoCorrect, you can also add words that aren't misspelled; they just aren't in the main dictionary. Like your name, your clients' names, your collaborators' names, names of cities, technical terms—anything that is spelled correctly can be added with just a click. From then on, AutoCorrect flags only the word if it is misspelled.

1. Right-click a red-underlined word to display the AutoCorrect QuickMenu.

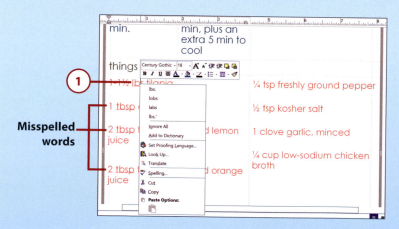

2. Click Add to Dictionary.

**You've decided not to
use a period after the
abbreviations here**

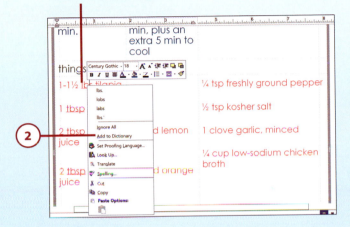

3. Right-click the other abbreviations and add them as well.

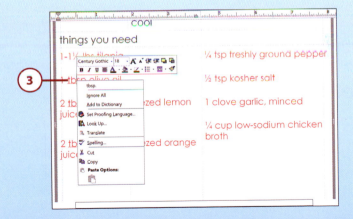

4. Save your work (as often as possible).

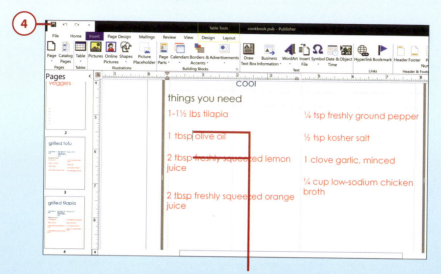

**Publisher no longer considers
the abbreviations misspelled**

Using the Spelling Tool

Regardless of your level of education or your background, your credibility will take a hit if you leave typos and/or misspelled words in your correspondence. You can avoid the embarrassment by running the Spelling Tool as your last step before printing or emailing.

1. Click the Review tab.

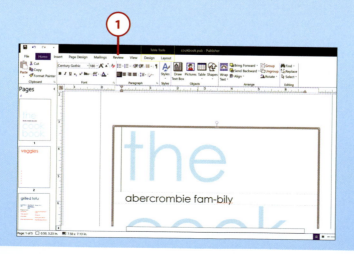

2. Click the Spelling command button to start spell checking.

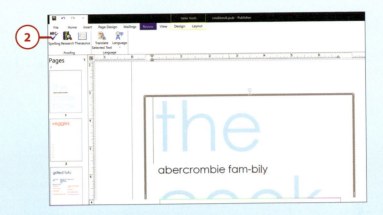

3. Click Add to add "bily" to the main dictionary.

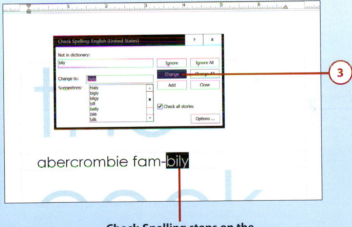

Check Spelling stops on the spelling of the word "family"

4. Click OK to clear the message box.

5. Save your work (as often as possible).

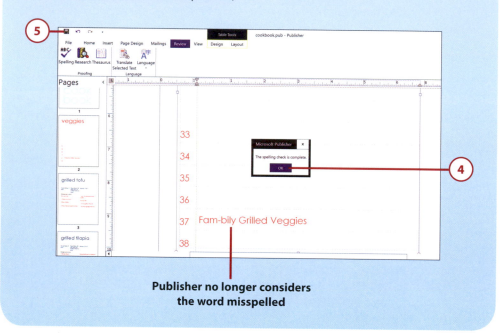

**Publisher no longer considers
the word misspelled**

>>>Go Further
TAKE CONTROL OF THE SPELLING TOOL

The Check Spelling dialog box holds more surprises! You can choose to Ignore a particular problem for just this one time, or for the rest of the publication. You can also elect to swap out the correctly spelled word for a misspelled word, throughout the publication.

The real power is in your ability to customize the spell check with the proofing options (see Appendix A). You can customize how AutoCorrect behaves. You can enable/disable options to ignore words in uppercase, words that contain numbers, Internet and file addresses, and duplicate words. Finally, this is where you can turn AutoCorrect on and off.

Working with the Thesaurus

A thesaurus helps you find alternative words to express yourself. Often we use the same word over and over, and wish there was a way to locate similar words. Publisher's Thesaurus looks up synonyms (words with similar meanings) antonyms (words with opposite meanings), and related words.

Looking Up Words

You can display the Thesaurus pane at any time; although if you select a word first, it looks up that word for you. If you did not, you can search for the word of your choosing.

When you do look up a word and a list of suggestions displays, each synonym is marked with a triangle. A right-angle triangle indicates that the synonym is expanded, revealing a list of similar words. A right-facing triangle indicates a condensed list of suggestions for that synonym.

1. Select the word you want to look up.

2. Click the Review tab.

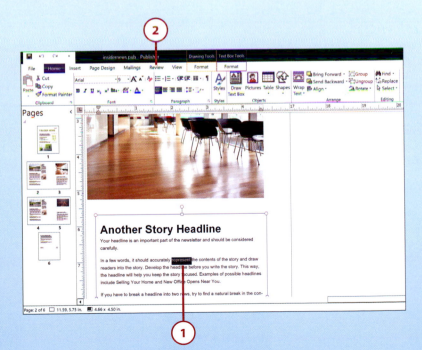

3. Click the Thesaurus command button.

4. Scroll through the list of suggestions.

5. Click a word in the list to look up suggestions for it.

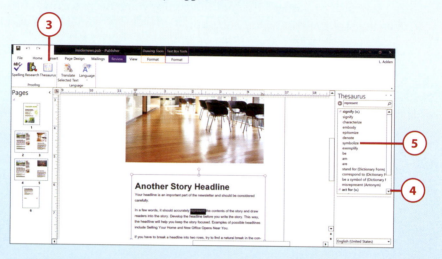

6. Continue clicking suggested words until you locate the one that fits.

7. Double-click the word to swap it out with the selected word in the publication.

8. Click the Close button to close the Thesaurus pane.

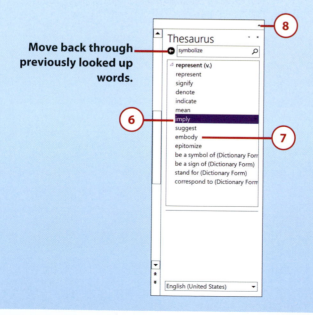

Move back through previously looked up words.

Expand Your Vocabulary

After you become familiar with the Thesaurus pane, use it to expand your vocabulary while you enhance the sophistication, or subtlety, of the wording in your publications. Even a dedicated bibliophile (book lover) can appreciate an electronic thesaurus.

>>>*Go Further*

SELECTING A PROOFING LANGUAGE

Writing in different languages involves more than just typing, displaying, and printing non-English characters. You also need to check spelling and look up words in that language in the Thesaurus. Type the text; then select it. Click the Review tab and then the Language command button. Click Set Proofing Language to open the Language dialog box. Select the language, and then click OK.

You can select additional options in the Publisher Options dialog box. Click the Review tab, and then click the Language command button. Click Language Preferences to display the Publisher Options dialog box with the Language option selected in the left pane. From here, you can add additional language modules to edit your documents. When you have more than one language installed, you can set a priority order for buttons, tabs, and the help topics.

In this appendix, you learn how to change the settings in Publisher. Topics include the following:

→ Setting the General Options
→ Setting the Proofing Options
→ Setting the Save Options
→ Setting the Language Options
→ Setting the Advanced Options
→ Customizing the Ribbon
→ Customizing the Quick Access Toolbar

Customizing Publisher 2016

Throughout these chapters, you have seen how Publisher offers a Custom option where you can create your own custom colors, for example. Custom color schemes are another feature where you can create your own customized set of color combinations.

The options for other aspects of Publisher are in the Publisher Options dialog box. You can open this at any time from the Backstage area.

Setting the General Options

The General options are for the certain aspects of the Publisher interface. You can elect to turn off the little pop-up Mini Toolbar that appears when you select text. (Although, I don't know why you would.) You can also opt to turn off the Live Preview option—perhaps because you have an older computer and it slows things down.

Miscellaneous items such as the username and initials used are here, along with fun stuff such as selecting an Office Background and Theme.

One item to notice is in the Start-up options section. If you prefer to start at the workspace rather than the New page, disable the check box.

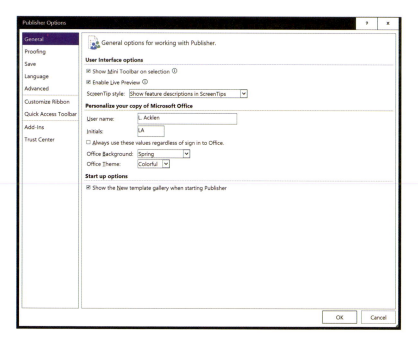

Setting the Proofing Options

The Proofing options enable you to customize AutoCorrect and Publisher's Spelling tool so that they both work exactly the way you want them to. AutoCorrect is particularly important because it makes corrections for you automatically. If you would rather it *not* do something, you can turn it off.

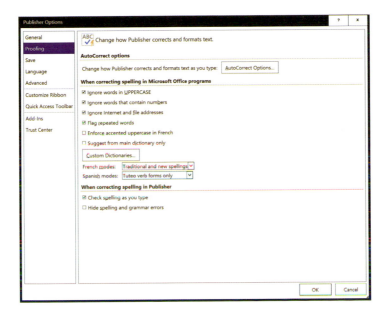

Clicking the AutoCorrect Options button opens up the AutoCorrect dialog box where you can customize the AutoCorrect features. One of the items to pay attention to is the list of automatic replacements. If you type outlines, every time you type "(C)", AutoCorrect replaces it with the copyright symbol (©). Removing this item from the list stops that replacement.

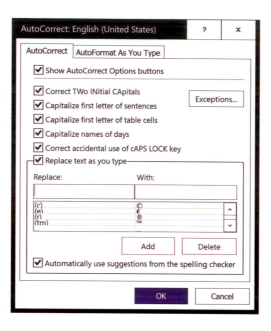

Clicking the Custom Dictionaries button opens the Custom Dictionaries dialog box where you can edit the main dictionary word list and add custom dictionaries so that they are used in addition to the main dictionary.

Setting the Save Options

The Save options enables you to customize how publications are saved in Publisher. The first option you see is the AutoRecover save interval. If you've never seen a message about recovered files, you've never known the magic of AutoRecover. Publisher automatically saves each open publication at a certain interval. If Publisher closes incorrectly and you are worried about losing your work, AutoRecover will have saved everything up to the save interval.

If you often forget to save your work, you should definitely decrease the interval so that Publisher saves for you, more often.

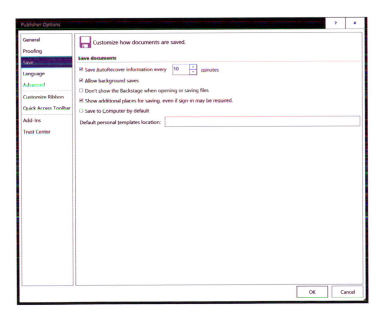

Setting the Language Options

The Publisher Language preferences are set in the Language Options page of the Publisher Options dialog box. Here, you can set the languages that you want to use when spell checking, grammar checking, and sorting. You can also set the language to use for the buttons, tab, and help topics in Publisher.

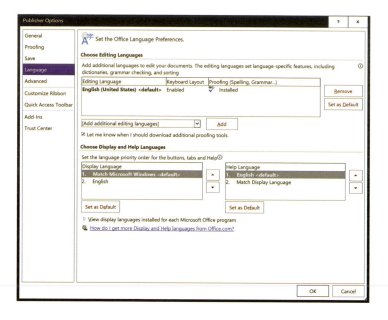

Setting the Advanced Options

The Advanced Options page has a long set of "advanced" editing options. They aren't actually advanced, but you can find a nice collection of items that can be enabled/disabled. Be sure to scroll down so that you can see all the available sections.

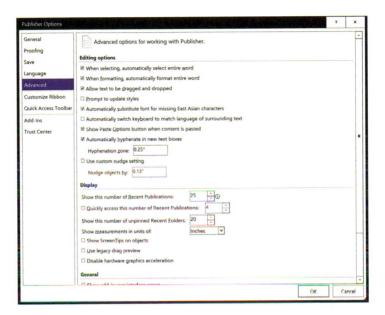

Customizing the Ribbon

You may have gathered from the name that this set of options customizes the Ribbon. And you would be right! The idea here is to move items from the left pane to the right pane to *add* them to the Ribbon. Moving them from the right pane to the left pane *removes* them from the Ribbon. Simply select a command; then click Add or Remove. Open the Choose commands from list to select another source from which to select commands.

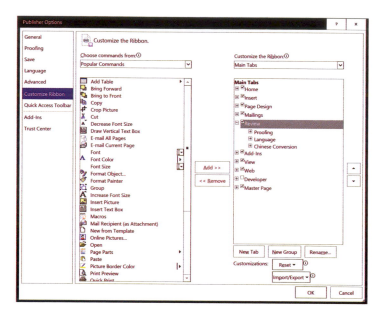

Customizing the Quick Access Toolbar

Last, but not least, the Quick Access Toolbar page uses the same method as for the Ribbon. You can add and remove buttons to put the commands that you use the most at your fingertips.

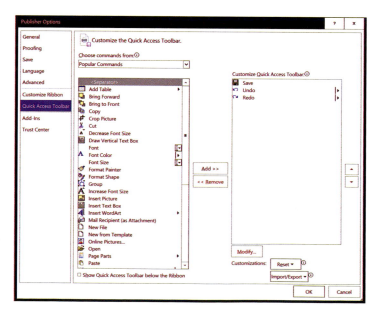

Index

G

H

I

S

More Best-Selling **My** Books!

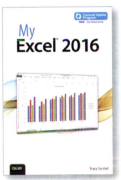   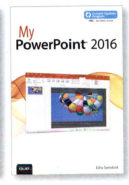

Learning to use your smartphone, tablet, camera, game, or software has never been easier with the full-color My Series. You'll find simple, step-by-step instructions from our team of experienced authors. The organized, task-based format allows you to quickly and easily find exactly what you want to achieve.

Visit quepublishing.com/mybooks to learn more.